77 NOTTS UNTIED

Eddie Neale
Michael Smout
Colin Bedford
Dick Williams

Lakeland, Marshall, Morgan & Scott, a member of the
Pentos group, 1 Bath Street, London EC1V 9LB.
Copyright © Marshall, Morgan & Scott 1977. First published 1977. ISBN 0 551 00787 7. All rights reserved. No
part of this publication may be reproduced, stored in a
retrieval system, or transmitted, in any form or by any
means, electronic, mechanical, photocopying, recording or
otherwise, without the prior permission of the Copyright
owner. Printed in Great Britain by J. W. Arrowsmith Ltd.,
Winterstoke Road, Bristol BS3 2NT. 776070L01

CONTENTS

NOTTINGHAM 77

Eddie Neale

It is difficult to think oneself back twenty years—and hopefully it will be impossible for some of you who read this book. But in Church terms it comes as a bit of a shock to remember what a small and beleaguered group Evangelicals were then. I was just leaving school and getting ready to join Her Majesty's Armed Forces as a foot-slogging, square-bashing private in the Sherwood Foresters, and the Suez crisis was looming large on the horizon. I remember Billy Graham had just visited Cambridge University for the first time, and the then Bishop of Durham, Michael Ramsay, had publicly voiced his fears about the effect that a visit of a tub-thumping, emotional, American-type fundamentalism would have on the bright young men of our future. In those days an Evangelical was someone who thought like Billy, had a fervour like Billy's and sometimes spoke a bit like Billy too!

But the tide had begun to turn. In the previous decade Scripture Union had collected a talented team of evangelists, and the crop of conversions from the camps and beaches of the country each summer was beginning to have an effect in the life of the Church, although many who went through an early conversion

1

experience turned later to other and more respectable forms of Church life. John Stott had produced a slim but scholarly book called *Men with a Message*, and there were others like the youthful Jim Packer who could hold their own with a university audience, and who were beginning to show that you did not have to throw all scholarship out of the window when you embraced this new fundamentalism.

Karl Barth was thundering from Germany, and C. S. Lewis was still throwing a few darts in England, but by and large the Church of England was Anglo-Catholic and liberal. Among the bishops Clifford Martin of Liverpool maintained a quiet evangelical spirituality and Cuthbert Bardsley at Coventry could preach as good a tub-thumping sermon as Billy himself, but both would have happily accepted the label of 'liberal'. The thought that an Evangelical might be a bishop or even an archbishop would have been laughed at. Evangelical clergy sometimes found it difficult to get a living, and in certain dioceses they were virtually barred.

Mind you, evangelical clergy were sometimes awkward customers to deal with. The ecumenical movement was enjoying its hey-day, but the University Christian Unions steadfastly refused to co-operate with people from different traditions, and the clergy often carried their entrenched attitudes into their parishes. They tended to be awkward over things like wearing stoles, and stuck to the 1662 Prayer Book in case some heresy crept in with liturgical revision. When the Archbishop of Canterbury first visited the Pope it was to the shaking of a great many heads. As a group, Evangelicals were against drink. If anyone smoked they had to do it secretly. Billy Graham's

2

wife, Ruth, caused ripples of concern when she confessed to using make-up! Their style was distinctly sober. Their men wore their hair short and their women wore hats. They viewed the theatre and cinema with suspicion, and they would have discouraged their young people from a career in the arts or journalism. They were equally suspicious of what they called the social gospel, and anyone who displayed too much enthusiasm for political or social issues might be regarded as 'going off the rails'.

Yet, along with all this, there was an intense faith in God which ran counter to the prevailing winds of scepticism and affluence. Because they were still unsure of themselves, Evangelicals were treading carefully. Billy Graham himself was accused time and time again of sweeping people off their feet by well-designed emotionalism. Because the evangelical leadership was sensitive to public opinion, they prevailed on the great evangelist to change his ways. In the end, Billy agreed to issue his famous appeals, 'I want you to get up out of your seat and come forward . . . ' without the emotionally charged singing of the choir in the background. But then complaints poured in that the sound of tramping feet created an emotional atmosphere much worse than the hallowed *Just as I am without one plea*. I remember the desperate efforts of the CICCU (Cambridge Inter Collegiate Christian Union) to avoid emotionalism. Their evening service cut everything to the bare minimum—no choir, no ceremony, no colour, virtually no singing, so that the evangelistic sermon finished up as very little different from an academic lecture from the pulpit.

Today the picture is very different. The National Evangelical Anglican Congress (NEAC) held in April

'77 at Nottingham University was a time for taking stock. One thousand, nine hundred and seventy-seven people thought, argued, worshipped, sang, enthused and slept their way through four days of Congress meetings to produce a statement which partially expressed the mind of Evangelicals today. What it doesn't say is that Evangelicals are stronger today in the Church of England than for a very long time. Both the Archbishops of Canterbury and York attended the Congress, and both Dr Donald Coggan and Dr Stuart Blanch would be happy to call themselves Evangelicals. That, in itself, would have amazed the Evangelicals of a previous generation. Bishops like David Sheppard of Liverpool and Maurice Wood of Norwich, bring a distinctive evangelical note to their episcopate. More evangelical young people are being accepted for ordination and there are more students in evangelical theological colleges than in any of the others. In the universities and colleges, the Christian Unions flourish as they have not done for many years, while the liberal and recently leftish Student Christian Movement has virtually disappeared.

Other changes were noticeable at Nottingham too. There are the minor changes like the women being more dressy and happy to look more attractive, while the men sport beards and jeans. Not only were very few dog-collars in evidence at Nottingham, but very few ties too. There wasn't even a ripple of excitement when it was announced that the bars would be open for half an hour before the meals, although the patrons tended to order halves rather than pints.

Perhaps the most obvious change is the number of people affected by the charismatic movement. All the

4

major meetings of the Congress were held in the enormous Sports Hall of Nottingham University. It really is a vast building, and the two thousand delegates looked a mighty army when assembled there, amid the clutter of the closed circuit television which relayed pictures to the late comers in the gallery. Monica Furlong, writing in the *Church Times*, says that the singing made a very loud noise. That is an understatement. At times it rose to a great roar. And from the Press Gallery, high at the back of the hall, looking down on the sea of hair on the back of two thousand heads, the surprising thing for me was to see hundreds and hundreds of arms raised in praise during each triumphant hymn. There were no charismatic excesses—apart, perhaps, from the woman who had seen a vision and was insistent on telling the session discussing the Roman Catholic Church all about it. But there were very large numbers of people whose faith was marked by a new warmth, and who sang and hugged one another with a new freedom.

One unchanging thing about Evangelicals is their heartiness. The All Souls' orchestra led the singing at the Congress, and they had obviously picked up some of the enthusiastic *bonhomie* of the vicar, Michael Baughen. It was he who led the final Communion service, when the urge to sing finally took over from the theologians. That had been one of the tensions throughout the Congress. On the one hand, the theologians delivering their weighty and sometimes boring theses, and on the other, crowds of Christians newly affected by the charismatic movement wanting to sing praises together. Michael Baughen captured their enthusiasm, and from the opening cry of 'The Lord is risen' throughout the two-hour long service

5

there was an intense spirit of victorious praise. The kiss of peace during this Communion took a good ten minutes. It was like a great reunion party, with people furiously shaking hands and greeting one another with hugs and kisses. On stage the Archbishop of Canterbury looked a little embarrassed and out of place as nuns and young bearded students, along with all those elegantly begowned choristers, embraced one another in the love of Christ. Instead of intercessions, the members of the congregation split into small groups of threes and fours and praised God together amid the hubbub. Up in the Press Gallery it was happening too, and only the less evangelically tuned reporters dived for cover. 'Why do they all wave their hands in the air?', asked the portly BBC Religious Correspondent. 'Have you heard of the charismatic movement?' came the reply. 'Really? Does that really happen here?' stumbled the BBC man.

In spite of the pleas during the sub-plenary sessions to bring Holy Communion back to the central place of the family life of the Church, it seems that not many evangelical clergy had come prepared for their Sunday Eucharist. When the conference organisers began to add up how many chalices they would need to administer wine to two thousand people, they issued a hasty memo asking any priest who had come with some Communion plate secreted in his cassock to help them out. Unfortunately, Evangelicals being what they are, there were very, very few of them who had brought their own chalice and paten with them, and several clergy who lived nearby went scuttling home to collect some silverware from their churches. In the end, Michael Baughen looked like a proud headmaster on Prize Giving Day, with the table weighed down by silver cups.

Another surprise for many of the delegates was to find that their preparation for the day's serious study was a presentation of street theatre drama. On both the Friday and the Saturday Breadrock filled the first three-quarters of an hour after breakfast with some fast moving sketches. Drama had come of age for the Evangelicals, although it was still of a hearty nature. There were some shepherds who were trying to think how to explain to their wives why they were hours late getting home. 'You know the missus . . . you could hardly expect her to believe that cock-and-bull story about ten thousand angels.' There was the inevitable Zacchaeus, climbing his step ladder, and an explicitly told tale of Dives and Lazarus. All good knockabout stuff which only partially revealed the talents which lay behind it. In fact, Murray Watts and Paul Derbridge are fast developing a real talent for drama. Murray took a first in English and History at Cambridge University, and at twenty-four had already tucked three major plays under his belt. During a break in the proceedings at NEAC he took his company down to the centre of Nottingham to act out their street theatre to the television cameras for a future production of 'Saints Alive' on ATV, and just that week he had written a hastily thrown together piece for Good Friday on ATV. It is one of the healthy signs of the renewal within the charismatic movement that drama is encouraged, and Breadrock have now joined St Michael's Church in York who will support them and allow them to continue their full time work in this field.

Murray is just one of the younger Evangelicals

deeply committed to the arts, and it was this new group who provided the first major revolt of the Congress. At Nottingham there were a good number of people who work full time as journalists, broadcasters, artists and dramatists, and their very presence fully vindicated the change in attitudes heralded at Keele ten years before. Of course, Local Radio itself was non-existent just ten years ago. At Nottingham there were at least twenty professional tape recorders in evidence. I suppose Local Radio had provided the wide open door through which many younger people with an interest in communications had entered.

There were other influences. With Rookmaaker preaching his gospel of the arts from Holland for all the devotees of Francis Schaeffer, and with the charismatic movement adding its hefty encouragement for crafts and drama, evangelical attitudes had done a complete turnabout. All these streams of thought have been brought together in London over the past few years in the Christian Arts Centre piloted by actor Nigel Goodwin, and it was from here that the revolt stemmed. His group of journalists and broadcasters include such able men as Andrew Quicke, one time director of 'Panorama' with Richard Dimbleby, and currently executive producer with a large independent newsfilm agency. Perhaps it was a mistake to ask Raymond Johnston, of the National Festival of Light, to produce the initial paper on the media to such a gathering. Broadcasters are sensitive animals, and thrive on praise. The NFOL is better known for its lambasting of the media, although Raymond Johnston came out of the chaos at Nottingham with flying colours in this respect. But the broadcasters thought the initial paper far too negative and set out to write their own. Michael Saward had the difficult job of trying to chair the session which finished in a shambles, with a large section of the Congress going off on their own to rewrite the paper. But the main thing to come out of the rumpus was this: that Evangelicals are now committed to the media in a way that could not have been imagined at Keele ten years before. It may be a direct reflection of their emphasis on evangelism which leads them to take this branch of the arts seriously. By contrast there are very few professional classical musicians, for instance, and only a tiny number understood Jim Packer's reference to blackberrying professors. If they had known their poets they might have done.

It is interesting too, that the lively discussion on the media showed up the paucity of the debate on the other ethical issues; politics, race, education, and global stewardship. In the final analysis each of these issues will prove to be a great deal more important than the manipulations of Big Brother.

Race was a case in point. Dr David Bronnert produced a carefully reasoned and low-key paper. Bronnert works in a multi-racial community in Southall, where he led the march for peace last year after an Asian youngster had been murdered—the biggest demonstration for racial harmony ever held in this country. He is deeply involved in the problems of race relations himself, and his paper was a masterly attempt to win support from a constituency who were not committed to the debate in a personal way. Some prejudices showed themselves in the discussion: 'It is difficult to accept when you see them getting better treatment over housing', said a young man from Islington. 'All the IQ tests show that they are below our standard of intelligence', said another young white man from South London. Bronnert took all these comments in his stride. He had been Chairman of the Evangelical Alliance Race Relations Group in its formative years, and was used to the response from the evangelical churches he visited. 'I find the responses vary enormously,' he told me afterwards. 'I remember visiting two evangelical theological colleges in the space of a few weeks, and getting completely different receptions. One was a college with a puritan tradition and so tended to work from Scripture rather than their emotions, and they gave me a very sympathetic hearing indeed.' He argues that the Bible speaks of migration and change, that the gospel is to do with breaking down the barriers between people of different races and backgrounds, and that you cannot believe in God while denying full humanity to a brother human being. But it is all presented in a deliberately low-key style. 'Sadly our evangelical Christians in the white suburbs will listen to quiet reason rather than our angry black brothers, and it is up to us to re-educate them in their attitudes. Many of their present attitudes are racist. I am appalled to see how many of our white Christians read the *Daily Telegraph* for instance. Of course, there is nothing intrinsically wrong with that, but the *Telegraph* was singled out by the Community Relations Commission as one of the worst for its biased reporting of racial issues. If our evangelical Christians are getting their information from that, then it is bound to be biased. Very few of them get their information first hand.'

It was left to a young, black, pentecostal social worker to rock the boat. Christian Weaver sensed the lack of urgency in the debate, and knew the pain that

10

complacent attitudes had brought to his fellow West Indians in Nottingham. 'Talk is not good enough', he said at one of the sessions. 'You talk about our disrupted family life, but you are the people who took our forebears into slavery. You messed up our history. You disrupted our families. And you now complain about us. It is you who need to repent.' This impassioned plea from one of the few black people at the Congress underlined the feeling that white evangelical Christians still mirror the attitudes of suburbia and are a long way removed from the action on issues like race.

But there was a genuine attempt at reconciliation. The strong feelings about Uganda were an illustration of this. One of the most welcome guests at the Congress was Bishop Festo Kivengere, who had escaped from Uganda by the skin of his teeth just a week or two before the Congress. He was greeted by prolonged applause when he stood up to tell the story of the death of Archbishop Janani Luwum. 'The grain of wheat cannot die without bearing much fruit,' he told the Congress, 'and our dear Janani did not die in vain. Many, even now, are being converted, and the Church is growing and praising God even in the midst of persecution.' Harry Sutton expressed the mood of the Congress as he hugged Festo Kivengere with tears in his eyes at the end of this speech. But when the Congress went on to vote that President Amin should not be allowed to visit this country for the meeting of Commonwealth Prime Ministers, it was noticeable that the key members of the CMS voted against it. Just a few hands raised in protest in the enormous hall. One of them, John Poulton, Secretary of the Archbishop's Council for Evangelism, said afterwards,

'It is so easy for a large Congress like this to pass such a resolution. But, in a way, feelings of revenge against Amin are sub-Christian, and do not reflect the respect with which the President is still held by many Christians within his own country. It is so much easier to pass resolutions like this than to do anything constructive for the black people in our own country.'

Each day of the Congress the *Church of England Newspaper* issued a mini-*CEN* which was waiting for the delegates as they took their seats for the morning session. It was, in itself, quite a feat of organisation, with an unruffled Chris Turner jumping in his car each evening with the copy and driving to Bletchley to get it printed. In one of the issues John King ran a banner headline asking 'What is an Evangelical?', and ended his tongue-in-cheek article by saying, 'The question of identity should be at the top of the list at NEAC. How can we know where we are going if we do not know who we are? What is an Evangelical? Tell us, somebody, please.'

It was left to the final session before anyone dared face that question. If the hectic discussions at Nottingham showed anything, it showed that there was no longer any one clean cut brand of Evangelical. In the end, it was John Stott himself who took up the challenge. Described by the *Church Times* as the Pope of Evangelicalism, and by others at the Congress as Chairman Stott, his personal influence over the proceedings was enormous. John Stott is now fifty-six, and as Rector Emeritus of All Souls, Langham Place, with the ebullient Michael Baughen as vicar, he is free to devote himself full time to the leadership of the evangelical movement worldwide.

At one time Stott was about the only Evangelical who was sufficiently respected in intellectual circles to lead university missions, and he stomped the campuses of our country with his particular blend of passion and theological clarity. Many of the younger breed of clergy owe their faith to his stirring presentation of the gospel during their time at university. And although his place as an evangelist has largely been taken by younger men like David Watson of York, who combine their intellectual abilities with the new fervour and open emotionalism of the charismatic movement which appeals rather more to the feelings of the younger generation, John Stott is still a welcome speaker. But his influence stretches much wider than that of a gifted evangelist. Stott is also something of a politician in Church circles. Naturally a rather shy and retiring man, he pushes himself into the forefront when he sees the need. It was he who started the Eclectic Society when he saw the need for change in the evangelical world, and recognised that it would only come as the younger men were given freedom to explore new ideas without the heavyweight older clergy breathing down their necks. So his society was for evangelical clergy under the age of forty, and it was a major factor in the new thinking now current in the evangelical Anglican world. At conference after conference, Stott encouraged the younger clergy to think afresh about the implications of the gospel to a changing world, while also encouraging them to hold fast to the Bible as the touchstone of their faith. It was no easy path, with radical and liberation theology raging on the one hand, and a retreat to biblical fundamentalism on the other, but Stott pioneered a new form of what he delights to call 'Bible Radicals' which is to be found virtually nowhere else in the world. More recently he has turned his attention to the Church worldwide, and was one of the growing number of Evangelicals represented at the last World Council of Churches Assembly. So that, at Nottingham, it was clearly John Stott who was the inspiration behind the proceedings and the man who steered the ship through some stormy waters to its final statement.

In a way, the Congress was a test of John Stott's continuing leadership of the new style Anglican Evangelicals. The reason John King was prompted to ask 'What is an Evangelical?' was simply that Nottingham displayed such a variety of views and attitudes that it seemed hardly possible to lump them all together under one label. But Stott has that rare blend of dictatorial strength and sensitive listening so that he not only held the Congress together but gave it a good deal of its cutting edge. Splinter groups and dissidents were encouraged to air their views, and then skilfully incorporated into the main body of the Congress, sometimes in late night sessions of personal reconciliation. In the end, the Congress had an appearance of unity that the pundits had thought impossible. It was at the very last session that John Stott set himself to answer the question. It is worth quoting some of his answer.

First, says Stott, Evangelicals are Bible people. 'Scripture is the inspired utterance, the written speech of God,' declared Stott. 'We deplore the arrogant attitude to Scripture common today, in which man sets himself above the Word of God. Evangelicals will want to develop an attitude of humility to Scripture, and place their intellects, their wills and their lives under the rule of the Bible.'

'But we are learning the need to be more thorough in our interpretation of Scripture', Stott went on. 'There are no easy answers in biblical studies, and perhaps the most important field of this study is associated with that blessed word hermeneutics.' Tony Thiselton's lecture on hermeneutics had become the standing joke of the Congress, especially for those who were impatient with the heavyweight academic theology of the study session. But many who were there would reckon this the most important part of the whole Congress. For the first time in a major gathering of Evangelicals Thiselton had opened up the possibility of critical studies, form criticism etc as being acceptable subjects for Evangelicals. Of course, this had been recognised for some time in the theological colleges, but it came as something of a shock for many people, clergy and lay people alike, to discover that their theologians no longer held rigidly to the historical accuracy of Scripture. In the afternoon session on this subject, there was a detailed question from the floor on the attitude of Jesus to divorce. 'If we accept', said the questioner, 'that a good deal of the New Testament reflects the teaching of the early church rather than being necessarily an historical account of the life of Jesus, and we know that the clause "save for adultery" is missing in some of the earliest texts, may we assume that this was an interpolation of the early church to give the authority of the spoken word of Jesus to the teaching of the early church? And, if so, what difference does this make to our modern debate about divorce and remarriage?' Thiselton simply thanked the questioner without attempting to answer the question. It

15

was a good illustration, he said, of the way in which the debate had moved on from the old fundamentalist controversy to new grounds. 'Your question is a perfect example of the kind of question with which we are wrestling today. That is where the action is.'

Not surprisingly the *Evangelical Times* had come out strongly against Thiselton's views on the authority of Scripture. But Thistelton insisted that Scripture did not answer every question. 'It does not give an authoritative archaeological picture of the size of Ninevah in the book of Jonah, for instance. We have to keep asking "What is Scripture authoritative *for*?".'

In the closing session Stott appeared to endorse Thiselton's approach. He shrugged off the jokes about hermeneutics (David Watson had referred to that well known German Professor, Herrman Neutic). 'Hermeneutics is simply the science of biblical interpretation', said Stott, 'and as Bible people we must learn how to learn from Scripture. At this Congress Evangelicals have begun the debate on hermeneutics. They take widely differing attitudes on these things, but what has impressed me has been the calibre of the debate. There has been a spirit of respect and love for those with different views, and this has been one of the hallmarks of this Nottingham assembly.

'But if we recognise first that we must be more rigorous in our interpretation of Scripture, we also recognise that we must be more radical in our application of Scripture.' He said that we should be conservative in our theology but not in our temperaments. 'Every aspect of our tradition as Evangelicals needs to come constantly under the scrutiny of

Scripture . . . so that our prejudices, our life-style, our patterns of church life and our resistance to change are being rebuked and reformed. A radical is someone who asks awkward and irreverent questions of the establishment. A radical is someone who goes to the root of things. And I believe we need to be radical in our approach to tradition, so that we become biblically-radical-conservative-evangelicals!'

Perhaps it is the question of hermeneutics which will continue the separation of Anglican Evangelicals from their brethren in the Free Churches. Since Keele there have been a good many words spoken and printed on the growing gulf between the two. One of the observers at Nottingham was Sidney Green, the young minister from Queensbury Baptist Church in Nottingham. He was one of the official representatives of the Baptists Union, but he was also conversant with the ways of Anglicans. He had been ordained first as an Anglican, and had served curacies in Skelmersdale and Carlisle before a tussle with his conscience brought him into the Baptist ministry. I asked him, after the Congress, whether he thought anything had been done to heal the rift between Anglican Evangelicals and Evangelicals within other denominations? 'In some ways I think it will be worse' he told me. 'They made the right noises of penitence about the rift in the closing sessions, but for the rest of the Congress there was virtually no notice taken of the Free Churches at all. I was amazed that in the discussions, for instance, about the shape of ministry in the Church that they took no account of the experiments within the Free Churches, who have been wrestling with these issues for very much longer than the Anglicans. My impression is that Anglican

Evangelicals have a rather overblown idea of their own strength at the moment, and it leads them into a sad self-sufficiency which ignores their brothers in other churches.' Certainly Nottingham did nothing which will help to heal the rift between the two groups, and perhaps now it is time for the Anglicans to stop talking between themselves and to share some of their thinking with a wider group.

So the Anglican Evangelicals emerged from a hectic four days at Nottingham with an immense agenda. All sorts of criticisms had been hurled about during a penitential self examination. They repented of their attitudes towards Roman Catholics in the past, and of their blinkered obstinacy. They regretted that there were not more women on the platform, and that lay delegates had not been more involved in the preparation of the Congress. They committed themselves to a more stringent review of some of the bigger social issues of the day, and regretted their lack of involvement with the social implications of the gospel in the past. But, in spite of all the notes of penitence, there was a swelling tide of confidence and self-importance in the life of the Church at large. Perhaps the kindest comments came, once again, from the *Church Times*. 'They have retained', said the Editorial, 15 April, 'a heartfelt and confident relationship with the Lord Christ, person to person. This is beyond doubt the greatest single factor in the Anglican Evangelicals' appeal to the 1970s. Their ecclesiology and theology may still look second-rate if not second-hand as compared to those of the Catholic and the radical movements in the Church of England. But Catholics and radicals alike have left on many the impression that they do not put the living Christ, as the Word of the eternal God, at the beginning, centre and end. A similar impression has been created by official gatherings such as the General Synod of the Church of England or the British Council of Churches.

'The religion of the Evangelicals feeds the souls of men and women because all the time it draws very directly on the inexhaustible power of the risen Christ. It is aware of the problems, but it is itself a part of the answer. The end-product is not more worry or doubt or confusion; it is not even discipline or duty. It is joy and peace in believing.'

WHAT IS AN
EVANGELICAL ANGLICAN?

Michael Smout

Evangelicals and Anglicanism

Evangelicals have never been great historians. What history most Evangelicals know centres round the story of the Reformation with Luther and Calvin as the star performers. What happened before and after that era is a glorious blank. It will be worthwhile taking a little time to look at the history of Church of England Evangelicals over the past three hundred years. This will help to put the Nottingham Congress in an important historical context. There are still lessons the Evangelicals can learn from their past history.

The Reformers called themselves *Evangelici* (Gospel Men). Since those days the term 'Evangelical' has described Protestant churches in general, and the Lutheran churches in particular. In England the revivalists of the eighteenth century were also known as Evangelicals. The Church as a whole had returned to one of its periodic times of slumber. One of the revival leaders was John Wesley, a Church of England clergyman. His followers attempted to return to the basics of the gospel. They were accused of too much enthusiasm. These were the Methodists, who later broke away from the establishment. Until recently it had been assumed by scholars that the times of revival stemmed completely from the Methodists. Recent historians, however, have shown that men such as William Romaine of Blackfriars, and John Venn of Huddersfield owed nothing to the Methodist movement. Yet they, and many others like them, were in the midst of the spiritual upsurge. They and their successors remained in the Church of England when the Methodists seceded. The ethos of Anglican Evangelicalism owes as much to them as it does to the Reformers. So the label 'Evangelical' became attached to a group within the Church of England distinct from the Methodists.

Nonconformists in Disguise

It is on the Anglican Evangelicals that we concentrate our attention. Many Free Church Evangelicals thought that the commitment made by their Anglican brethren at the Keele Conference of 1967 to the Church of England was something quite new. They had always been regarded as nonconformists in disguise. This was quite true of the past twenty or thirty years, but was certainly untrue of historic Anglican Evangelicalism.

Those who remained in the Church of England at the end of the eighteenth century were not simply men who did not have the courage of their convictions to leave, or even those who thought the Church 'a good boat from which to fish'. They were rather men deeply committed to the Church of England as well as being Evangelicals. Typical of them was Charles Simeon, arguably the outstanding Anglican Evangelical of that era. In 1783 he was appointed as vicar of

21

Holy Trinity Church, Cambridge, where he ministered until his death. From Cambridge he exercised an immense Evangelical influence not only in the university city itself, but throughout the country. His fifty years at Holy Trinity covered the transition from Evangelicals being very unpopular in the Church of England until the time they were the most influential group. During his early days of ministry the seatholders of Holy Trinity walked out of the church. They took care to lock the doors on the pews so that no one else could use them. When Simeon tried to put seats in the aisles, the churchwardens threw them out into the churchyard. So it was that for ten years Simeon's congregation had to stand throughout the services. It was a comment on how Evangelicals were considered by the rest of the Church when a contemporary wrote, 'Those who worshipped at Trinity were supposed to have left common sense, discretion, sobriety, attachment to the Established Church, love of the liturgy, and whatever else is true and of good report, in the vestibule.' But by the end of Simeon's time at Cambridge, the distinguished Lord Macaulay was writing, 'If you knew what his authority and influence were, and how they extended from Cambridge to the most remote corners of England, you would allow that his real sway in the Church was far greater than that of the Primate (Archbishop of Canterbury).'

Simeon also hit upon an effective way of spreading Evangelical influence in the Church of England. With some money he had inherited, he bought, as was possible in those days, a number of livings. This meant that he was able to say who would be vicar in those parishes. Naturally enough he appointed

Evangelicals. Other Evangelical laymen followed his example and soon the Simeon Trust was formed, which today still appoints to a number of livings up and down the country.

Nineteenth-Century Superiority

It is now generally recognised that Evangelicals were at the height of their influence in the Victorian Church of England between 1830 and 1850. It is estimated that during this period evangelical clergy made up between a third and a half of all the parochial clergy. Here was strength indeed. But it was not the clergymen of the period who have stuck in the mind. It is two laymen whom most people remember. The first was William Wilberforce. Through his association with the Clapham Sect, a group of Evangelicals with a burning social conscience, he became involved in many good causes. But his place in history is assured by his leadership of the fight to abolish slavery. Wilberforce's place as the leading evangelical layman in the country was filled by Anthony Cooper, the seventh Earl of Shaftesbury. Like Wilberforce he was engaged in a breath-taking range of social work, but is best remembered for his fight to improve conditions for the factory workers resulting in the Ten-Hour Act of 1847 and the Factory Act of 1874. More significant for his influence on the Church of England, was the fact that he happened to be the brother-in-law of Lord Palmerston, the Prime Minister. Palmerston was not particularly interested in the Church of England, or any church for that matter. So when it came to appointing bishops, Palmerston went to Shaftesbury for advice, and more often than not took it. The net result was that in the 1860s there were more Evangelicals on the bishops' bench than ever before. The first to be appointed was Henry Ryder of Gloucester, followed by men like Bickersteth of Ripon, J. T. Pelham of Norwich, and S. Waldegrave of Carlisle. But the peak success of all was the appointment of John Bird Sumner as Archbishop of Canterbury. In 1848 Sumner was given this position by Lord John Russell, the Prime Minister, to check the rising Tractarian movement. But although generally popular, Sumner was not a good leader, and his failure had an influence on the later Evangelical decline.

Rising Damp

The decline of the strength of Anglican Evangelicals after the middle of the nineteenth century was slow but sure. For those who believe in learning the lessons of history, there are things to be learned from this decline of which the Evangelicals in the second half of the twentieth century need to take due account. For while Evangelicals were at the peak of their influence, the seeds of decay were already apparent for those who had eyes to see.

The first factor which Evangelicals did not grapple with until it was too late was the growth of the Oxford Movement. When they did come to grips with it, they tackled it in the wrong way altogether. The Oxford Movement of the 1820s was, as its name implies, a new impetus which started particularly in Oriel College, Oxford, amongst a small group of brilliant intellectuals. Although it had its roots in the high church party of the seventeenth century, it was greatly influenced by the great revival of interest in the glories of the medieval past. As the Evangelicals had claimed to rediscover the truths of the Bible through the interpretation of the Reformers, the Oxford Movement claimed the same rediscovery through the interpretation of the early church fathers. Owen Chadwick in his book *The Mind of the Oxford Movement* claims that 'like the Evangelical Movement it was more a movement of heart than head'. This statement is not entirely true. Indeed both movements were of the heart. But the leaders of the Oxford Movement had a lot more head behind the heart than did the Evangelicals.

The leaders of the Oxford Movement were men of great intellect and intelligence. It could be claimed that some of them were in the genius class. The greatest of them all was John Henry Newman closely followed by Edward Pusey, Richard Froude and John Keble. These were theologians of the first rank whose perception and insight were great enough to have an influence for the next century or more. They were creative theologians not content to repeat or glue together other people's work, but to produce a vision of theology unheard of before. As with most new movements it took a number of years for the work of the cloistered theologians in the university to filter down to the rank and file. But although altered in certain peripheral ways, the essence of the work of the early Oxford Movement led into what became known as the Tractarians (after the tracts written by Newman) and later the Ritualists (because of the ritual introduced into the services of the churches). It is today better known as the Anglo-Catholic movement.

25

The Evangelicals had nothing in comparison with the giant Oxford theologians. Perhaps the only one who could come even within shooting distance was William Goode, who supported the evangelical Philpotts' baptismal controversy with Bishop Gorham of Exeter. It is interesting to note that in a recent evangelical publication, *The Dictionary of the Christian Church*, no nineteenth-century evangelical theologian rates an entry, i.e. space is given to Newman, Pusey, Froude, and Keble. Here then was a critical evangelical weakness: its lack of first rate theologians. As time went on the movement simply became sterile because there was no fresh thinking or creative work. Therefore its impetus came to a standstill. Hence when Ritualism became a force in the land, the Evangelicals had to resort to force of law rather than force of thought. The Church Association was formed to combat the opposition. Some Ritualist clergy were taken to court and a few spent time in prison. Not unnaturally this sort of action only served to increase support for the Ritualist cause. This was the opposite effect from the one the Evangelicals wished to achieve.

The lack of creative evangelical theology was also evident in the stance they took up on issues which were being raised by the new age of scientific enquiry which cast doubt upon some of the accepted truth of the Bible. Evangelicals automatically went on the defensive and rather than attempt a creative theological re-construction, decided to put up the barricades and shoot down all invaders. This decision meant that a massacre was inevitable. The name associated in most people's minds is that of Charles Darwin and his theory of evolution. But the appearance of Darwin's

Origin of Species in 1859 was only the climax of a whole series of geological and historical investigations which began to throw doubt on the evangelical approach to the Bible. Again the basic problem was that there were no evangelical theologians of outstanding quality to grapple with the new crisis, and the day was lost.

Decline and Decay

From the middle of the nineteenth century onwards the evangelical decline was inevitable. Party strife increased and Evangelicals put themselves in opposition on principle to anything anyone else in the Church of England said. They became increasingly sectarian, steering well clear of anything which might compromise the true faith.

The best known evangelical bishop, John Charles Ryle (Bishop of Liverpool 1880–1900), was in fact an anachronism, born fifty years too late. The re-issuing of much of his work by Banner of Truth, the Puritan press, has given many the impression that Bishop Ryle was a Free Churchman who somehow became a bishop in the Church of England. But as books like *Knots Untied* show, he was deeply committed to the Anglican Church and sometimes was as outspoken against Nonconformists as he was against the Church of Rome. When Church Congresses, forerunner of the Assembly and then Synod, started, Ryle was the first Evangelical to become involved, much to the dismay of many of his fellow Evangelicals and the thunderings of the Protestant weekly newspaper *The Record*. Ryle was accused of being a compromiser and a 'Neo-Evangelical'. His evangelical adversaries

27

could not stand the fact that he associated with Anglo-Catholics and the like. But Ryle was an exception to the rule. He was a moderate Calvinist, committed to that historical tradition in the Church of England. He had no time for the Keswick Convention with its particular doctrine of sanctification and refused to appear on its platform.

From the turn of the century Anglican Evangelicalism was a movement which confined itself to the parishes. Here, secure in the freehold, the vicar could to all intents and purposes not be moved until he wanted. The decreasing number of Evangelicals were content to see the Church of England as 'a good boat from which to fish' and get on with the job of preaching the gospel. The appointment of bishops such as Handley Moule of Durham were few and far between. Two things happened during the first half of the century. First of all, there was a stronger alliance between Anglican and Free Church Evangelicals. The alliance had been there for a number of years, as expressed in the Evangelical Alliance founded in 1846, but finding themselves increasingly uncomfortable and despised in the Church of England, Anglican Evangelicals naturally found their greatest solace and comfort in those who similarly held the great evangelical doctrines of grace and salvation. So the Keswick text of 'all one in Christ' became a rallying point for Evangelicals across the denominational barriers.

The Free Church Evangelicals could never quite understand how their brethren could be Evangelicals and remain in the corrupt Church of England with its especially peculiar doctrine of infant baptism, but none the less they were prepared to put up with them. Secondly, the Anglican Evangelical attempts to keep the Church true to the 39 Articles were constant and determined.

A number of Church Missionary Society members felt that the Society was becoming too liberal in doctrine and broke away to form the Bible Churchman's Missionary Society. Then in 1928 an alternative prayer book was presented to Parliament for approval. Evangelicals felt that it was unacceptable because of some of its teachings, and a combined effort of clergy and prominent laymen saw that it was defeated.

Sons of the Reformation

These Evangelicals felt that they were very much the true sons of the Reformed Church of England. A beleaguered garrison maybe, but no one was going to turn them out of their rightful inheritance. There are not many of this vintage left now, and those who are, are naturally in the older age bracket. Their doctrine centred round the 39 Articles, unchanged and unaltered for three hundred years. Their worship centred round the Prayer Book. Their reading was limited to the King James Version of the Bible. In public they were recognisable by deep dog-collars, that loudly said, 'we are Evangelicals'. James Insight in his recollections *I Turned My Collar Round*, remembers how at deanery chapter meetings the Evangelicals were the ones in the sports jackets as opposed to the regulation black of the Anglo-Catholics. Their faith was a world-denying one in that it was negative rather than positive. No smoking, drinking or dancing were more important than enjoying the many things of life that God had given to be enjoyed, such as music and books. I can clearly remember the shock I had when, as a fresher at university, I saw the prayer secretary of the Christian Union smoking a cigarette. I could but wonder if he was a backslider in need of counsel.

It is perhaps easy to ridicule these Evangelicals of a former generation, but they were only victims of their previous history. It is difficult to see what different course they could have taken. They were perhaps more effective than we realise. Such warriors as Guy King of Christ Church, Beckenham, Kent, reached many people for Christ. The sadness was that many of those who were converted considered their Evangelicalism only an adolescent faith. To go on to maturity, one had to leave Evangelicalism behind. Hence many who started off in the evangelical fold found its narrowness and anti-intellectualism too much. It seemed to have nothing left to offer, and so many became liberal churchmen of various hues. It would be surprising if present-day Evangelicals were being any less effective in evangelism than their predecessors were. The difference now is that it is possible to go on in the Christian faith, exploring all its avenues and possibilities and remain an Evangelical.

All our Yesterdays

A personal memory in the previous section will have given due warning that we have reached the period of recent evangelical history in which in a small way the writer has been involved. It was in the 1950s that Evangelicalism began to spring to life once again. I was brought up in a small village in Herefordshire where I played the organ in the small village church.

In that peaceful rural setting, the politics of church life were remote. My own spiritual experience began when I joined the RAF for the then two years compulsory National Service. I met a Christian who introduced me to Jesus Christ as a real and relevant person. Even then I knew nothing of the term Evangelical or its implications. My faith did not seem to suffer overmuch from this lack.

My ecclesiastical innocency began to pass when I graduated to Oxford University and was introduced to the OICCU (Oxford Inter Collegiate Christian Union). The CU was mainly Anglican, and many of the speakers who came for the week-ends were Anglican too. They were significantly a bright new rising generation of men. There was John Stott, of All Souls, Langham Place, David Sheppard of the Mayflower Centre, Canning Town, Michael Green, a curate from Eastbourne, Maurice Wood, vicar of Islington, John Collins, vicar of St Mark's, Gillingham, Raymond Turvey, vicar of St George's, Leeds, and James Packer and Alec Motyer of Tyndale Hall and Clifton, Bristol. There was hardly an old man amongst them. They were the vanguard of the evangelical resurgence.

The church which Christian Union members were expected to attend was St Ebbe's, under the leadership of Basil Gough. It was considered tantamount to treason to attend the nearby St Aldate's, where Keith de Berry was vicar, since this was considered somewhat too liberal.

A large proportion of the Christian Union members were entering the ministry. Up till then it had been almost automatic to go to either Wycliffe Hall, Oxford, or Ridley Hall, Cambridge. Now the great attraction was in the two Bristol theological colleges, Tyndale and Clifton (now combined into Trinity College), situated on either side of the Downs. Here the students sat at the feet of Jim Packer and Alec Motyer, and Bristol became the launching pad to send bright young ordinands into the ministry of the Church of England. Second to Bristol, came another conservative evangelical college, Oakhill, situated in London. Here an older evangelical scholar, Alan Stibbs, had a great influence.

The Christian Union at this time was still very much an independent body. Its relationship to such bodies as the SCM (Student Christian Movement) was very much that of the Jews and the Samaritans. Christian Union members were rarely seen in the college chapel, and took little part in the life of the college as a whole.

I felt God calling me personally to the ordained ministry. Following the usual practice of looking round a number of theological colleges as a prospective student, I went first to Ridley Hall, Cambridge. Here, during evening prayer in the chapel, I remember standing firmly unmoved as the rest of the college turned to the east for the Creed. In those days that sort of thing really mattered. In my interview with the principal of the college, then Cyril Bowles (now Bishop of Derby), I was very disturbed about his view on the authorship of various biblical books. Therefore Ridley was deemed unsound, and I went to look round Tyndale Hall, Bristol. This I concluded was very sound in doctrine, but did not seem quite exciting enough. In the end I opted for the London College of Divinity (now St John's, Nottingham). This was mainly because it was in the process of changing from a liberal to a conservative evangelical college. I felt it part of my duty in life to help this process along. The architect of this change in outlook was Michael Green, by far the most dynamic personality on the staff, who as principal later on was responsible for moving the college to Nottingham.

The Phoenix Rises

These were exciting times. The Evangelical phoenix was rising from the ashes. Resurrections usually centre round key personalities, men who can inspire their followers to greater things. The years from 1955 to the Keele conference of 1967 and beyond were dominated by what would now be considered the 'old brigade'. The two most influential of these were John Stott and Jim Packer. All Souls, Langham Place, had for many years been as much the citadel of Evangelicalism as All Saints, Margaret Street, had been of Anglo-Catholicism. A city centre church, it catered mainly for an eclectic gathering of students, young professionals and visitors. Here, after the war, came John Stott as curate, to become vicar a few years later. He rapidly became widely known as a Bible expositor, preacher, evangelist and writer of rare quality. Whereas London-based Evangelicals would previously need to go to Westminster Chapel to hear the hour-long sermons of Dr Lloyd Jones, now somewhat shorter expositions were available at All Souls. Anglo-Catholics tended to deride 'John Prot, of All Stoles', and those in the evangelical circle were able to imitate the voice and mannerisms of the famous preacher. It was rumoured that John Stott's influence was so great that by sitting behind a pillar it was impossible to tell whether the master or one of his curates was preaching.

John Stott

The Stott influence was immense. He came to be regarded as the uncrowned archbishop of the Anglican Evangelicals. His small book *Basic Christianity* became a classic in its own time. Very few evangelical clergy prepared their confirmation courses without it. In evangelism, Stott was in great demand not only in the universities of this country, but throughout the world. His writing showed the results of great productivity and much research rather than originality. But as an English equivalent of William Barclay, he had the gift of conveying in simple terms some of the profundities of evangelical faith.

Possibly it will be neither as preacher, writer nor evangelist that future historians of evangelical history will see his role. His influence is behind, in one way or another, most of the forward moves of evangelical church policy which will be noted later. Although this has been more of an unseen, unsung task, it has been the marshalling together of the evangelical ranks towards a concerted policy which has been the keynote of the Stott contribution. He has opted to be actively involved in the Church of England scene in general. He has preferred to leave matters like General Synod to his followers. Content to provide the strategy and let others be seen in the front line positions he has remained over the past twenty-five years, simply the Rev John Stott. It is more likely that he has refused a move to the episcopal bench than that he has not been offered one. Amongst the company of bishops, there is no doubt that he would have been outstanding, possibly reaching York or Canterbury. Some would feel it a pity, with the lack of outstanding Evangelicals involved in the Church as a whole, if he had refused a bishopric. On the other hand there is no doubt that, even since Michael Baughen succeeded him as vicar of All Souls, he has exercised an influence in the evangelical movement which might have been lessened considerably by duties and involvements as a diocesan bishop.

Jim Packer

Besides John Stott, the influence of Jim Packer was as great, but seems to have diminished considerably over the past few years. Arguably the theological heavyweight of the Evangelicals, Packer introduced the works of the Puritans to a whole new generation of Evangelicals. With a doctorate in the work of Richard Baxter behind him, he was mainly responsible for making Evangelicals once again think theologically. After the lightweight Arminian theology of the Keswick movement, here was something into which his knowledge-thirsty students could get their teeth. Second-hand bookshops were searched from top to bottom for the out of print works of John Owen, Thomas Watson, William Gurnall and the other Puritan writers. Here was a Puritan renaissance indeed. The issue which divided the evangelical theological colleges was whether a person was a Calvinist or an Arminian.

The Christian Union Executive Committee, of which I was a member at Oxford, chose its speakers with great care. If they were suspected of being Arminians in their outlook they were not acceptable.

Calvinists of the calibre of Herbert Carson of St Paul's, Cambridge, and Bertie Rainsbury of Emmanuel, Croydon, were. It needed a visiting missionary to remind me that the primary qualification of a speaker was not so much whether he was Calvinist or Arminian, but whether he was full of the Holy Spirit.

When Banner of Truth began to produce cheap reprints of the Puritan classics, they became more easily available to avid evangelical readers. Bookshelves were overflowing with bulky volumes, which were not actually read but seen as a status symbol. This Puritan period passed fairly quickly. Although giving a solid theological basis, it was not really relevant to the contemporary needs of a fast changing Church of England. It can be sensed that the passing of this era has left its leader, Jim Packer, sitting a trifle uneasily amongst the wreckage, as the main course of Evangelicalism has gone off in another direction.

Other names from the era of evangelical resurgence are worthy of note because they are still amongst the present leaders. One is Colin Buchanan who became the 'whizz-kid' of the time. Arriving as a member of the staff of the London College of Divinity and surviving its move to Nottingham, he has made a name for himself as one of the Church of England's leading experts on worship. In addition, he is the publisher of the widely respected Grove booklets which have maintained a steady production of contributions by Evangelical writers on all sorts of subjects connected with the relevance of evangelical Christianity today. Another, Michael Baughen, the Rector of All Souls, Langham Place, has been responsible for much of the new musical exuberance which has come through the production of *Youth Praise* and *Psalm Praise*. Sir Norman Anderson, Professor of Legal Studies in London University, is the outstanding evangelical layman and has received due recognition by being elected Chairman of the House of Laity in General Synod.

Recognition at Last

So since the mid 1950s, evangelical influence has dramatically increased in the Church of England. This influence can be indicated in a number of ways. Until fairly recently, any commission set up to study a matter of importance in the Church would not have a conservative Evangelical amongst its representation. This revealed what the rest of the Church felt about their merit and importance. In fact most of the rest of the Church hardly realised that they existed at all. The only Evangelicals of any repute were those of the liberal variety, as represented by the great tradition of Max Warren, Douglas Webster and Bryan Green. The liberals believe many of the same things as the conservatives but not quite so dogmatically. For example, they believed in the atoning death of Christ, but not necessarily the substitutionary theory; they believed in the authority of the Bible, but not the infallibility; they had a rather subdued doctrine of hell, preferring a God of love to a God of justice. But at last the conservative Evangelicals were convincing the Church of England that they did exist in their own right and could be ignored no longer. Now it would be unimaginable for any commission to sit without a conservative Evangelical representative.

The recognition by the Church as a whole of

Evangelicals is also seen in a number of appointments of Evangelicals to high office over the past few years. The first notable achievement was the filling of the bishopric of Norwich by Maurice Wood, then principal of Oakhill Theological College. This came as a surprise even to Evangelicals on three accounts. First, Maurice Wood was felt by many to have been too blatantly an Evangelical with his 'old-fashioned' approach to evangelism. Then, he had not made a notable contribution to the Church of England in general. To make his appointment even more surprising, Norwich was a predominantly Anglo-Catholic diocese. Then came the appointment of David Sheppard, the Warden of the Mayflower Family Centre in Canning Town, as Bishop of Woolwich. He was already nationally famous as an England cricketer and hence his work was followed with great interest in more than just evangelical circles. He became known at the Mayflower for his practical research into the problems of the urban church. In addition he also took a strong stand over the apartheid issue in South Africa. Both concerns helped towards his appointment as Bishop of Woolwich in 1969 by the Bishop of Southwark. In 1975 he succeeded Stuart Blanch as Bishop of Liverpool on the latter's move to be Archbishop of York. It is generally felt that Bishop Sheppard will finish up as either Archbishop of York or Canterbury.

True-Blue Evangelicals

Some would consider the removal of John Taylor from being General Secretary of the Church

Missionary Society to be Bishop of Winchester as another success for the Evangelicals. This indicates some of the difficulty of distinguishing conservative and liberal Evangelicals. Bishop Taylor has always stood in the liberal tradition. In its exuberance, the Keswick Convention invited him, amongst others, to speak at the Centenary Celebrations of that four-square Evangelical body. A controversial talk by the bishop made sure that they would never invite him again, although many Evangelicals secretly applauded what the bishop said about evangelical involvement in the world.

It is galling, if understandable, constantly to meet people of other churchmanship who simply do not understand that the liberal and conservative evangelical traditions are connected, but quite separate. How then is it possible to describe a conservative Evangelical? John King in his paperback *The Evangelicals* gives his description of the 'true-blue' Evangelical. 'The Islington Conference is clearly true blue, so is the Church Pastoral Aid Society. But beyond this opinions will differ. Simeon's Trustees will probably be recognised as acceptable, so will Church Society. (Indeed there are those who will leap to point out that Church Society is the citadel of Anglican Evangelical orthodoxy).) Among the missionary societies the Bible Churchman's Missionary Society and the South American Missionary Society will be unquestioned. But the Church's Ministry among the Jews? and Lee Abbey? An entire spectrum is involved—a spectrum ranging from the Protestant Truth Society and the Fellowship of Evangelical Churchmen at one end of the scale to Ridley Hall and Lee Abbey at the other.

'Clergymen are placed on the spectrum, absurd though this may seem to the layman, according to their dress, whether they invariably wear a scarf and hood, or whether they are prepared to wear stoles or even the entire eucharistic vestments!'

Further signs of increasing evangelical strength have been the number of Evangelicals elected to General Synod and the revitalisation of the *Church of England Newspaper* as a crusading organ for fresh evangelical thinking and initiatives. This happened primarily under the editorship of John King, though suffering financial difficulties it seems to have lost its initial impetus. It is interesting to note that a considerable number of Evangelicals have switched their newspaper allegiance to the *Church Times* now that it is less of a militant Anglo-Catholic journal than it was in days past.

Most of the roots of the evangelical renewal stem back to an organisation now known as the Universities and Colleges Christian Fellowship, but better known as the IVF (Inter-Varsity Fellowship). This movement co-ordinated the work of the Christian Unions in the universities of this country. Although interdenominational in outlook, many of the new Anglican Evangelical leaders owe much to their IVF connection in their spiritual development at university. Behind the IVF itself lay the major vision of Douglas Johnson, for many years its General Secretary. Self effacing to the extreme, few ever saw him or spoke to him outside the inner circle. But this one man and the movement he vitalised was essential to the evangelical revival in the fact that the new Evangelicalism stemmed very much from the universities and their Christian Unions.

The Keele Water-shed

The great Keele Conference of 1967 was seen as a water-shed in modern evangelical history. Here at a gathering of some 1,500 clergy and lay-people, evangelical euphoria reached its height. There was a new determination to be henceforth committed to the Church of England and to play a full part within it. It was a gathering full of hope and confident of the future.

Now, ten years later, we have had the Nottingham Conference of 1977. This writer came to the gathering of 2,000 delegates hoping that the history of the past ten years would be examined critically and realistically and that this review would set the course for the next generation or so. The *Church Times* reporter at the Keele Conference had stated that 'Their (the Evangelicals) new image has been beaten into shape by 1,000 people in three gruelling days'. Was it possible that the same would be true of Nottingham?

In some ways the past ten years have been successful. Numerically, among the Church of England clergy, Evangelicals are stronger than they have ever been. In spite of the decline in the number of ordinands, the evangelical theological colleges are full and it is thought that evangelical ordinands make up a third to a half of the total number. Surely no one can ask for more than that. But it is at this point that we need to look back to the lessons of history as outlined earlier on. The signs of the seeds of decay are as evident for those who have eyes to see as they were last century.

Scarcity of Scholars

In the first place, it is disappointing after twenty

years or more of evangelical upsurge that there is such a lack of scholarly theologians who might be termed of first division status. Reliance is still greatly placed upon rehashing other scholars' insights. A look around the university theological faculties gives little cause for optimism. The one outstanding university professor, F. F. Bruce, the Rylands Professor of Exegesis at Manchester University, is a member of the Christian Brethren and now reaching the end of his career. Oxford and Cambridge have tended to produce the country's leading theologians, but there the faculties are very much dominated by non-Evangelicals. It is significant that the radical movement which may well turn out to have greater staying power than the evangelical one, was inspired by a theologian, John Robinson. He was and is a top rank Cambridge theologian, whose notorious brief spell as Bishop of Woolwich was but a brief interval in a brilliant academic career.

A glance round the theological college staffs is just as dismaying. Here are people who would normally be expected not only to teach, but to spend vacations in doing research and producing books. Instead we tend to receive a diet of popular paperbacks.

A recent plea that theological college staffs be urged to spend more time producing work which would make non-evangelical theologians sit up and take notice may help solve the problem. But one cannot help thinking that it may be more a question of quality rather than time available. Hopes were raised in the early 1960s that Latimer House would serve this purpose. Set up in Banbury Road, Oxford, as an evangelical research centre, its intention was to give scholars just the time and solitude they needed to produce works of theology. So far it has not really managed to do this. This is partly because the staff over the years have found themselves heavily committed to servicing study groups, writing pamphlets, giving lectures and in general being busy about most matters except the actual purpose for which the House was founded. Also it is doubtful if all the staff appointments were wise ones. It is sad that out of all the essays in the Nottingham preparation books, *Obeying Christ in a Changing World*, the only one which seems to be creatively new is that entitled 'Understanding God's Word Today', by Tony Thiselton, a lecturer in Biblical Studies at Sheffield University. Here is a brilliant attempt to take the traditional evangelical view of the authority and interpretation of the Bible and shape it into something new yet still loyal to the old. The essay breathes an atmosphere of theological creativeness which is not very apparent elsewhere.

South-Bank Religion

A second connected criticism of Evangelicism over the past decade is that it has failed to address itself to the theological viewpoints of others in the Church with any urgency. For example, there has been a grave underestimating of the strength of radical theology stemming from the likes of Paul Tillich and Dietrich Bonhoeffer and being interpreted for a British audience by John Robinson. Many Evangelicals thought that the bombshell of *Honest to God* was but a storm in a tea-cup which would soon pass by. They failed to recognise the importance of the South-Bank theology and the fact that it would take at least ten years to filter through to ground level. The radicals have been concerned to make Christianity relevant to the ordinary man. They are convinced that up till now we have been trying to answer questions people are not asking. What people really want to know is if Christianity has anything to say to the world of work, politics, the third world and humanity in all its need.

Now it can be argued that Evangelicals have noted what the radicals have been saying and taken steps to right matters. For instance, the preparatory book for the Keele Conference, *Guidelines: Evangelicals Face the Future*, had only a twenty-page chapter by Sir Norman Anderson on the Christian view of the world. By comparison the whole of one of the three Nottingham books is devoted to the subject. This is commendable and much to be praised, but what has not really been grappled with what radical theology denies as well as affirms. In its emphasis on the humanity of Christ, it denies his divinity. To make people 'fully human' in Christ is indeed to concentrate on the example of Christ, yet it undervalues his death for sin on the cross. For radicals, to evangelise is to solve human problems by means of encounter groups, political action, or the like. Everything is in human terms. The miraculous, including the need for personal conversion, is denied. In trying to show the rightful humanity of Christ, his divinity is often denied, thus resurrecting an ancient heresy in modern clothing. Unfortunately there is no sign whatever of a fruitful dialogue commencing between radical and evangelical theologians. The churchmanship division today is not so much between high and low churchmen, as between those who believe in the supernatural and those who do not. The Nottingham books pay hardly any attention to this field of joint

44

theological exploration.

I have recently had several long discussions with some who hold a radical theological viewpoint. It would be difficult for those who made up the 2,000 strong show of evangelical strength at Nottingham to believe that many radicals do not even know that Evangelicals exist, and if they do, have no idea what they believe. When the belief that the Bible teaches that people need to become new men and women in Christ is voiced, the response is frequently wide-eyed amazement that anyone could think such a thing in the twentieth century. Now I am glad to say that I count a number of radicals as personal friends. The reason that radicals and Evangelicals have so few dealings with each other is partly the fault of both. Some radicals have about them the air of confident arrogance which was typical of most Evangelicals until fairly recently. This involves thinking that their point of view is 100 per cent right and everyone else's 100 per cent wrong. On the other hand, so far too few attempts have been made by Evangelicals to have meaningful dialogue with radicals. This is a gap which rapidly needs to be filled.

In this respect it is significant that the one big theme joke of the Congress was the word 'hermeneutics' which is the theme of Tony Thiselton's essay. For example, David Watson, the vicar of St Michael's, York, told the story of the student who thought that hermeneutics was the name of a German theological professor. Behind every joke lies a truth. The truth here was that theological terminology is a foreign land to the average Evangelical. It was impossible not to feel that the Congress felt that this was the way it ought to remain.

The Congress spent a lot of time in sackcloth and ashes being repentant for the sins of the past. Although a worthy thing to do in moderation, the great desire to avoid triumphalism (i.e. blowing our own trumpets) left the Congress sometimes being less affirmative of what is good in the recent history of Evangelicals than it might. Unfortunately one of the few trumpet-blowing exercises occurred when the Congress Statement said (A.10) 'We thank God for the increase of evangelical biblical scholars in recent years. What is now needed as well are systematic theologians and specialists in ethics, who will help us develop an integrated Christian world view.' This is true in a small way, but to the initiated it might sound as if the evangelical world was swimming with modern day Augustines and Luthers. Unfortunately a statement much nearer to the real state of affairs is that of a *Church Times* writer, 'Their ecclesiology and theology still look second-rate if not second-hand as compared to those of the Catholic and radical movements in the Church of England.' 'Second-rate and second-hand' may seem strong, even insulting words to use of evangelical theologians, but an obvious example of this is the essay on 'Global Stewardship' in book three of *Obeying Christ in a Changing World* by Philip King, who is General Secretary of the South American Missionary Society. Theologians of other traditions have been spelling out the theological basis of the stewardship of the world and its resources for the past twenty years or more.

Organisations such as Christian Aid and the World Development Movement have been putting the theology into practice. Hence an example of evangelical theology desperately trying to catch up to the point where other Christians have been for many years. Praise has been heaped on Evangelicals because the footnotes of the Congress books show a wide reading of other people's theology. This is indeed very necessary and to be welcomed, but again it is just a case of catching up to where other theologians are. The real search should be for evangelical theologians of such a calibre that they are able to advance the theological debates on all issues on an equal footing with theologians of other traditions. Hopefully the Congress Continuation Committee will make a priority in coming to grips with the gaps in our scholarly ranks. Not to do so will be to face the certainty of evangelical disaster.

Christian or not Christian?

The Congress itself clearly illustrated the unawareness of the strengths and weaknesses of other theologies within the Church of England. An illustration of this was the Congress section on 'Jesus Christ is Lord' by Dr J. I. Packer, Associate Principal of Trinity College, Bristol. Dr Packer has been mentioned earlier as one of the people who had a great formative influence on the evangelical revival in the Church of England. In reading his essay in the first Congress book, it seemed that his material had changed very little over the past twenty years. To be fair, some pages of his essay (pp. 48–55) deal with humanitarian doctrines of Christ, but there is little sense of the urgency of the present theological situation. The session led by Dr Packer at the Congress which I attended, turned into a lay-persons' guide to

47

the heresies concerning the Trinity, again using illustrations which I remember from many years ago. The problem here for Dr Packer may well have been a tension that ran throughout the Congress. Most of the lay-people present had little theological knowledge and wanted simple explanations. Naturally most of the clergy (estimated at one-third, but they seemed a lot more) wanted something a little more advanced. This turned into an unresolved debate as to whether the Congress Statement should be in plain man's language or to impress theologians.

None the less, Dr Packer did talk for a little about present-day radical theologians and how widely separated his views were from theirs. But the important issue he never seemed to tackle. If radicals deny the divinity of Christ and consequently bodily resurrection, miracles, judgement and the second coming, in what sense can we recognise them as Christians? To raise such an issue would be to open Evangelicals to the accusation of causing disharmony and disruption in the Church of England. Perhaps it would do the new-found image harm. I have a feeling that Evangelicals are so fearful of saying anything which might cause other sections of the Church not to like us, that we are afraid to speak plainly on certain issues. In fact the Congress Statement on 'Jesus Christ the Lord' is a disappointing one. But to its credit its one reference to other theological views does say (B.2) 'the widespread present-day view that the New Testament confession of Jesus Christ as God incarnate is a myth concerning a mere man is a real, if unintended, denial of Christianity'. For my money it is the most important sentence in this section's statement and ought to be pondered at great length.

The fact that evangelical theology is far behind its experience was illustrated on a number of occasions during the Congress. During one of the evening worship meetings, Alec Motyer decided to treat us to a very long exposition of part of Deuteronomy. Unfortunately he missed the boat altogether, for the 2,000 people gathered in the hall were looking for spiritual stimulation after a hard day's work in study sessions. What they received was very unexciting and quite tedious. But the biggest condemnation of the exposition was that no attempt was made to apply its theme of obedience to today's Church and world. We were simply told to be obedient. The delegates went away asking how. The exposition was timeless in the sense that it could have been given in 1877 as much as 1977 so little was there any practical application.

Sainsbury and Sin

It is significant that it took an optional workshop on urban mission to produce any signs of a significant evangelical theology which remained committed to historical theology but re-interpreted it.

Roger Sainsbury of the Mayflower Family Centre, Canning Town, London, had written a paper for the workshop entitled 'Gospel for the City'. In it he states 'Evangelicals in the past have looked at sin in mainly individual terms but now are seeing sin at social and individual levels. Sin has affected man, society and the whole of creation. I find it hard to agree with Jim Packer that "the world's deepest problems are individual problems" if he sees problems and sin related.'

Another statement of Roger Sainsbury's opens up a theological issue which became of increasing importance as the Congress went on. He reminded us that part of the Keele statement was that 'the atonement can be fully understood only when Christ is bearing the penalty of our sins in our place. This is the deepest, though not the only significance of divine love demonstrated in the Cross.' He then went on, 'Evangelicals of the 1950s and 1960s of which I was a product, held fast to the doctrine of the substitutionary atonement AND I still do. But increasingly I have begun to see the Cross as demonstrating other aspects of divine love, focusing all that Jesus came to do and also highlighting the full extent of the sin of the world.'

Here was raised a question concerning the fundamental evangelical doctrine of the substitutionary nature of the cross. Historically this interpretation of the cross has been the controlling factor of other aspects such as being an example of the love of Christ. The section of the Congress Statement under 'Jesus Christ the only Saviour' states (C.I) 'Regarding the Atonement, we all gladly affirm that the death and resurrection of Jesus is the heart of the gospel of salvation. Christ died for our sins in accordance with the Scriptures, and was raised on the third day. Nevertheless, we give different emphasis to the various biblical expressions of Atonement. Some see the truth that Christ died in our place as the central explanation of the cross, while others who also give this truth a position of great importance, lay greater stress on the relative significance of the other biblical pictures.'

This statement reveals a difference of opinion which occurred in the sessions led by Michael Sadgrove and Tom Wright, who were responsible for the

50

essay in the Congress book. Were the conservative Evangelicals simply turning into old fashioned liberal Evangelicals? The mark of the liberal Evangelicals has always been to hold similar doctrines to the conservatives, but not quite so definitely. So the liberal has always wanted to play down the substitutionary nature of Christ's death. The debate reflected a justifiable fear that slowly but surely Evangelicals are changing their doctrinal ground. It must have come as a relief to many to read in the Congress Statement 'Understanding the Bible Today' that 'We reaffirm our belief in the divine inspiration of Scripture, its entire trustworthiness, the sufficiency of its teaching for salvation and its unique authority.' Here at least the ground had not changed.

All of this reflected fears that Evangelicals no longer stood firm on the essentials of the faith. Hence the draft resolution, passed by an overwhelming majority in the final plenary session, requested that 'In the light of current theological speculation and scepticism, as illustrated during this Congress by the TV programme "Who was Jesus?", we call on the Archbishops publicly to confirm that the Church of England still stands by its historic faith in the Christ of the Scriptures and the Creeds.' Here was a positive statement that our basic convictions need re-emphasising. The explanation in the introduction to the statement that 'much Evangelical conviction is taken for granted' is simply not good enough.

Non-Anglican Evangelicals

The Congress as a whole put Evangelicals in the mainstream of Anglicanism even more than the commitment at Keele did. But before we assess what this

51

means, we need to look briefly at what this implies for non-Anglican Evangelicals. The years between Keele and Nottingham have seen increasing strains upon relationships. The Anglican Evangelicals seemed to have thrown in their lot with the Church of England to the complete exclusion of Free Church Evangelicals. After Keele an abortive meeting was held between leaders of both groups. Annual meetings of the Evangelical Alliance have raised the question, and that is about all. Anglican Evangelicals have seemed remarkably more concerned with the Church of Rome than anyone else. Meetings have been held with 'charismatics' to talk over matters of concern, but the Free Church Evangelicals have been left out in the cold. The fault has not just been on the Anglican side, for some Free Church brethren have seemed content to withdraw and sulk.

At the beginning of the Congress the issue was again noticeable by its absence. But a conviction grew as the days passed by that this lack of family feeling could not be allowed to continue. This conviction became concrete when the Declaration of Intent declared 'In grief we find ourselves at a distance from our Evangelical brothers in other denominations, we undertake to seek closer fellowship and co-operation with them in informal consultation, in shared worship and in united outreach.' It is important that this intention be turned into action and that the Evangelical Alliance, for example, sponsor consultation amongst the leaders of the two groups.

Tell It as It Is

The questions they will have to tackle are hard ones, for although some of the teaching held in common binds the two groups together, there is much that does not. Churches such as those belonging to the Federation of Independent Evangelical Churches are growing in strength. Their teaching and communication of it to the contemporary world has not changed much over the past few hundred years. Yet the certainty of the faith which they proclaim has a ring of authority which seems to be attracting people to their churches. It looks as if the decade which was very much anti-authoritarian may be giving way to one which wants some of the answers rather than a continual stream of questions. 'Tell me about your faith, I have enough doubts of my own' may become the watchword of the next ten years. We may be learning our lesson too from the steady increase of Jehovah's Witnesses in this country. This success again is mainly due to the fact that they are saying something definite, however defective, about their faith. Anglican Evangelicals ought not to be too worried if other sections of the church object when the definite fundamentals of the faith are stated without fear or favour. For example, Margaret Duggan in her review of the Congress in the *Church Times* says, 'All the heart beating did not entirely disguise the touches of triumphalism in some of the attitudes. The Evangelicals are very sure they are right about many things, and that in their scriptural tradition they are asserting the official position of the Church of England.'

The Anglican Evangelicals can learn from their Free Church brethren not to be over-sensitive about such accusations.

Roman Catholics

At the other end of the spectrum let us look briefly

at evangelical relationships with the Roman Catholics. There seem to be three schools of opinion amongst Evangelicals. The first would not even go as far as the Congress statement in 'seeing ourselves and Roman Catholics as fellow-Christians'. They raise the question of 'What is a Christian?' and find that official Roman Catholic teaching still refutes the doctrine of justification by faith. They note that the leading Roman Catholic radicals such as Hans Kung are not acceptable to the hierarchy. At the other extreme, the charismatic movement has united Roman Catholics and others across church barriers. They have experienced deep fellowship in Christ in spite of sometimes almost radically opposed official church teaching. The problem is working out how to reconcile their experience with their theology. Much work remains to be done on this area of study. In between the two extremes lie probably the majority of Evangelicals. The Congress statement reflects their willingness to explore the ground further, but raised some important questions which could bring these explorations to a full stop. To ask 'does the Roman Catholic Church place itself under the Old and New Testament Scriptures as its final authority under Christ?' is surely to invite the answer 'No'. Whatever other ground seemed to shift at Nottingham, the final authority of Scripture remained a firm rock.

The Future

Having touched on relationships with Free Churchmen and Roman Catholics, we turn attention to the future of the Evangelicals in the Church of England. As the days of the Congress went by it became evident that this crucial question was to be avoided if possible. What is an Anglican Evangelical? While they were not committed to playing a full part in the Church of England it did not really matter. But now it does. The question was raised in 1969 in a booklet entitled *Evangelical Structure for the Seventies* by Colin Buchanan. In a section headed 'Who are Anglican Evangelicals?' he points out that there are three different reasons for Evangelicals being Anglicans. Some are born Anglicans and feel at home in the Church for no particularly theological reason. Others are Anglicans because they feel that the 39 Articles and the historical formularies of the Church are basically evangelical. Unfortunately for them this position has been so eroded over the years that to hold to it can only be an illusion in the present comprehensive state of the Church of England. The third position is that which is based on a doctrine of the Church. 'Although they hold that the Church ought to confess sound doctrine, says Buchanan, 'they view this as much as an ideal to which they are working as an historic position from which the Church is departing.' He then re-emphasises that 'the difference is ultimately one about the doctrine of the Church', and adds, 'the task of Evangelicals in the Church of England is in desperate need of re-appraisal from a doctrinal standpoint.' Over the following years little has been done about this 'desperate need'. There is still no carefully thought out Anglican Evangelical doctrine of the Church. And Nottingham did little to provide one.

The section in the Congress Statement under the heading 'The Church as Institution' was a great disappointment in this respect. Here Tim Dudley-Smith, the Archdeacon of Norwich, had a great opportunity to give this subject a good airing. Unfortunately, he missed it. The only points where evangelical involvement in the Church of England was touched on at all were in such statements as 'We support a careful use of theological training resources in providing for a diversity of needs. We nevertheless believe that the true comprehensiveness and well being of the Church will be better served by the continuance of the distinctive theological traditions of existing colleges than by any attempt to impose a uniform comprehensiveness. For the different traditions within the Church of England to make their contribution in charitable and fruitful dialogue each must have a firm base in colleges, and also in parishes and voluntary societies.' This statement was in response to the Guildford Report on *Theological Training*; *A Policy for the Future* which had felt that since 'most of our (theological) colleges were founded about a century ago at the height of party controversy in the Church of England the time had come to get rid of churchmanship'.

This response was excellent as far as it went, but the logical question to follow was what, then, is the role of the Evangelical in the Church of England today? Is churchmanship a dead issue or not? Tim Dudley-Smith's contribution to the Congress really did not face this important issue head-on. Many of the matters considered in the statement on 'Church as an Institution' are indeed important ones, such as the need for flexibility in institutional structures, upholding 'the Church of England ideal of a resident ministry' and the call for applicants who want to become Church of England members to 'make some current declaration of the Christian faith'. But these are issues, like many others in the Congress statement, which are not specifically evangelical viewpoints. They are not necessarily any the worse for that, but here was a great opportunity missed to evaluate the distinctive evangelical contribution to the Church.

Anglican Evangelicalism Defined

It is difficult to imagine what the Evangelicals would do without John Stott to act as their anchorman. Early in the Congress he responded firmly to the suggestion that the tag 'Evangelical' was no longer needed and that Evangelicals simply needed to call themselves Christians. He felt that only when all of the Church of England could call itself Evangelical would it be time to drop the name. He also pointed out that he saw being an Evangelical as a higher priority than being an Anglican, hence the name of the gathering, the National *Evangelical Anglican* Congress. He obviously felt it important to spell out such issues, and to resist the temptation of the Congress in all its euphoria to forget its roots. In the final plenary session of the Congress, he again returned to this same theme. This time his response was to a question which was raised by John King, ex-editor of the *Church of England Newspaper*, in the daily Congress edition of that paper. His short article is worth quoting in full because it raises what could be the vital dilemma of the Evangelicals over the next few years.

'A crisis of identity has arisen at Nottingham. People are asking "What is an Evangelical?" and very few are coming up with a satisfactory answer. Many delegates are arguing that it is time to drop the labels and merge into the mainstream of Anglican Church life.

'Others argue to the contrary; nowadays there are more Evangelicals than ever, power and influence are with the Evangelicals. It is a respectable label to wear. The question came up at a Press conference when John Stott was bluntly asked, "What is an Evangelical?" Slightly dazed, he replied that an Evangelical was a Christian who placed submission to the authority of Scripture prior to all else. "Is that all?" asked a disappointed reporter.

'The fact is definition of the Evangelical position is becoming harder as the lines of demarcation in our Church get ever more blurred. Is it Nottingham's task to give an answer to delegates in doubt? Can the Steering Committee and the powers behind the thrones give a straight answer to a straight question "What is an Evangelical?" Hundreds of delegates would go home happier if they knew the answer without having it wrapped up in incomprehensible jargon. The question of identity should be at the top of the list of NEAC. How can we know where we are going if we do not know who we are? What is an Evangelical? Tell us, somebody, please.'

Stott to the Rescue

This was the question that John Stott tried to answer in the final Congress session. He spoke of the 'distinctive convictions we cherish' and which 'we must not surrender'. He stated that first of all Evangelicals are Bible people. Although the official Anglican position is based on the authority of the Scriptures he called Evangelicals to be more conscientious in their study and more radical in their application. Also he saw Evangelicals as Gospel people. On the basis of the saving events of history, God made all things new, giving a new freedom and a new society. The Congress chairman obviously thought it was important to make this concluding statement as an attempt to hold Evangelicals together in a cohesive movement.

The danger throughout the Congress had been that the participants would leap on their horses and ride in all directions at once. To achieve this unity was a remarkable effort upon the Congress chairman's part. The danger of a rapidly expanding movement is that it will fragment into small pieces. But John Stott managed to weld past Evangelical tradition to the new and adventurous thinking taking place.

The question now is, how much longer will he be able to do this? It was surprising that no one challenged John Stott's assertion that the priority order is Evangelical first and Anglican second. The implications of such a statement are vast for the future of Evangelicalism in the Church of England. To say that the name Evangelical ought not to be dropped until everyone calls themselves Evangelicals is to state that Evangelicalism is not just one of a number of traditions in the Church of England, but is in fact true Anglicanism. This means that Evangelicals are still very much a party however much Anglo-Catholicism and other traditions have valuable insights.

Sir Norman Joins In

Sir Norman Anderson said during the final Congress session that he did not like to think of Evangelicals as merely a party but as a party with certain fundamental traditions. This was a slight toning down of the situation, fitting well with an interview in the *Church Times* in which Sir Norman said that although still a conservative Evangelical, he felt it right to withdraw from evangelical positions of responsibility when he became Lay Chairman of General Synod. This was so that he could be seen to be impartial. This well illustrates the tension between being an Evangelical and an Anglican. It would be interesting to know why non-Evangelicals in General Synod would be more likely to think that Sir Norman would be an impartial chairman if he resigned his evangelical offices. In this respect it was fascinating to hear of an Evangelical who recently was turned down for an important post because it was felt that he would see everything through evangelical eyes.

Too Keen

All of this in a way reflects the distrust which others in the Church of England have for Evangelicals, although some Evangelicals would like to think otherwise. Experience seems to teach that Evangelicals are acceptable when they are saying things which the rest of the Church have been saying for years on such matters as global stewardship, the media, marriage and so on. It is as if others are delighted that at last Evangelicals have come to their senses and are thinking like they do. It is only when Evangelicals talk about their fundamental convictions such as the need for evangelism and winning people for Christ, that others say they do not want to know. 'Evangelicals are great folk, but we do wish they would stop harping on about conversions and new birth' seems to be the attitude. But, of course, if they keep growing up, then one day they will lay aside these childish views.

Evangelism as understood by Evangelicals is still a divisive factor in the Church of England. If evangelical leaders are too strong on it, they will not get promotion. Those Evangelicals who do get promoted as archdeacons, deans and bishops are those who are not so noted for their evangelistic fervour, but for other no doubt worthy qualities more acceptable to the Church at large. Those who appoint are unlikely to risk another appointment such as Maurice Wood as Bishop of Norwich. He is probably too fervent an evangelist for that diocese to cope with. It is also likely that Michael Green would have been a bishop by now had he not been so keen on winning people for Christ. His abilities as administrator, scholar and writer are far above a number of those on the present episcopal bench. His fault is that he is too good an evangelist.

Evangelicals are constantly priding themselves on their growing strength in the Church of England. This may be true at parish level, where there has always been strength. It is by no means as true in non-parochial ministries and in leadership positions.

Evangelical Deserts

There are large areas of church life where it is difficult to find Evangelicals. In Church House, Westminster, the Church of England administrative centre, it is hard to find any Evangelicals. Here are the headquarters of the Board of Education, Social Responsibility, Mission and Unity and others. Evangelicals do not walk corridors of power. All the dioceses have industrial chaplains, children's officers,

61

youth officers, and adult education officers. The same story, few Evangelicals. There is a remarkable ignorance too amongst Evangelicals of what others in the Church of England are doing. During one of the sessions at the Congress, a small group formed to discuss the problem of unemployment. Since it included the North-West organiser for the Job Creation scheme, there was no shortage of expertise. But it became obvious as the discussion proceeded that some present unconsciously felt that they were the first in the Church of England to consider such a topic. There was a complete oblivion that the Board of Social Responsibility had done a tremendous amount of work on the subject over the past few years.

In the Lead

If Evangelicals are conspicuous by their absence in non-parochial ministries, there are not a lot more of them in positions of leadership in the Church. At first sight this is not too obvious, for the *Church Times* claims that 'at present the Archbishops of Canterbury and York are both race horses out of this stable'. This sort of statement shows the tendency of non-Evangelicals to put all Evangelicals in a lump. They do not recognise that historically there has been a liberal and conservative evangelical movement. Dr Coggan belonged to the conservative evangelical camp when a travelling secretary for the then Inter Varsity Fellowship many years ago. He later moved into the liberal sphere. Dr Blanch has never at any time been associated with the conservative Evangelicals. Having made that clear it leaves Bishops Wood of Norwich and Sheppard of Liverpool as the evangelical representatives on the episcopal bench. Unfortunately for the Congress Bishop Sheppard was absent in the United States, and Bishop Wood was recovering from the effects of trying to walk through a plate glass door. So the Congress was shorn of its only two stars from amongst the diocesan bishops. There are forty-three dioceses in England so two out of that number can hardly be said to be a preponderance of Evangelicals. A recent survey showed that twelve of the diocesan bishops were trained at Westcott House, an Anglo-Catholic College, and four at Cuddesdon, which is of the same hue. Altogether twenty-five of the bishops were trained at Anglo-Catholic colleges. This predominance is even heavier when suffragan bishops are considered. Each diocesan bishop is able to appoint his own suffragan (deputy) bishops to assist him in his diocese. In number they are just under sixty. Of these twelve were trained at Westcott House and ten at Cuddesdon. Overall nearly half were trained at Anglo-Catholic colleges. This is not to say that all these men are not good bishops. It is simply a warning to Evangelicals not to think that a number of archdeacons of evangelical flavour scattered round the country means that they have a grip on the leadership of the Church. Of course there may be one or two more evangelical diocesan bishops to come. Timothy Dudley-Smith, for example, is an obvious contender. But there is no sign of evangelical predominance ever being as great as that of the Anglo-Catholics.

Anglo-Catholicism

It is curious that the Anglo-Catholic movement has

been written off as a back-number. And yet there is a case for saying that they are still a very powerful force. It is significant, for example, that Anglo-Catholic diocesan bishops have no qualms about appointing Anglo-Catholic suffragans as their assistants. Not for them the business of saying 'To be fair, we must have a balance of churchmanship and therefore have non Anglo-Catholics as suffragans.' Also, note ought to be taken of the fact that many of the key city-centre parish churches, such as Leeds and Liverpool, are of the high-church tradition. It would be unwise therefore to write the Anglo-Catholics off. It could well be that over the next ten years the Evangelicals will shoot their bolt. Even now, while the whole Church is singing the praises of the evangelical resurgence, it could be that the Anglo-Catholics are in fact a more potent force.

Which all brings us back to where, more or less, we came in. Are Evangelicals going to learn the lessons of history? To do so will mean a lack of contentment with quantity of numbers and a genuine search after quality. But it could well be that the Nottingham Congress marked the zenith of the movement, and later historians will be able to trace a subsequent decline. The problem is that the seeds of that decline in the lack of first rate theologians will not become obvious for another ten or fifteen years and by then it will be too late.

It will be easy for self deception to take place. John King has never been given to euphoria about the evangelical movement but in the *Church of England Newspaper* he becomes positively ecstatic. 'Evangelicals may not yet have solved all their own problems or those of the Church and Society' he says, 'but this

Congress was clear evidence that they have gone forward purposefully from Keele and have the ball at their feet. It is difficult to see how such a movement can fail to put its imprint decisively on the Church of England and to begin to influence English society during the next ten years.'

The *Church Times* was also enthusiastic about the Evangelicals in a way which would have been impossible not many years back. 'The religion of the Evangelicals feeds the souls of men and women because all the time it draws very directly on the inexhaustible power of the risen Christ. It is aware of the problems, but it is itself a part of the answer.'

But is the evangelical movement completely aware of its problems? If the above comments have seemed a little negative and off-key amidst a sea of enthusiasm and excitement, then there are two positive suggestions to make. One is that Evangelicals need to pray for an outstanding theologian on the doctrine of the Church to arise soon, very soon in fact. Unless this happens the tension between being an Evangelical and also a member of a comprehensive Church could split the movement wide open.

The more Evangelicals commit themselves to the Church of England the more of a problem this tension becomes. The old pragmatic answer that we belong because the Church of England is a 'good boat from which to fish' will no longer do. The other more theological answer that we belong because the basic formularies of the Church, for example the 39 Articles, are the Reformation position will no longer do either. For one thing the Church in practice is blatantly far from the Reformation position, and for another it is assumed that the Reformers were

Evangelicals as we know them today. Of course they were not, and the present evangelical movement owes as much to the eighteenth-century Evangelicals as it does to the Reformation. Evangelicals need urgently to start working on their doctrine of the Church.

Secondly, if history is not to repeat itself, Evangelicals need to strengthen their structures within the Church rather than weaken them. The Nottingham Congress does not mean that the network of the Church of England Evangelical Council, Regional Councils, and Diocesan Evangelical Unions needs loosening. Rather it needs to be tied tighter. There is still a need for such 'party' organisations as Church Society and the Church Pastoral Aid Society. Why are people afraid of the word 'party'. Perhaps because it smacks too much of politics. 'Tradition' sounds a less harmful word. But whether party or tradition, Evangelicals will need a sound base to work from, otherwise it will become a diffuse movement which will eventually fade away.

MISSION, MINISTRY
AND UNITY
Colin Bedford

The Need for Evangelism

It is perhaps very significant that the emphasis on
evangelism and mission was not obvious in the three
preparatory books for the Congress. In recent years
our Church of England seems to have spent a great
deal of time looking at worship, canon law, finance
and similar matters. Evangelicals often appear to be
following in the same ways, and a very timely challenge was issued to all of us on the first evening. Some
of the respected leaders, for example Jim Packer,
Harry Sutton, Gavin Reid and Gordon Landreth
issued a statement which regretted the lack of
emphasis on evangelism and reminded us that obedience to the Great Commission (Matt. 28: 19) is a
universal obligation on all Christians. It reminded us
that every church should see evangelism as a primary
responsibility, and that the Lausanne Covenant is a
sound basis for understanding that responsibility.
Their statement shows the step forward in positive
thinking since Keele when it went on to say 'that
Christian social action makes visible the power of
Christ and that acceptance of social responsibility

may not be divorced from evangelism'.

They have reminded us that we need 'evangelists' to assist us in the urgent task of evangelism in our nation, where the majority of the population is not now being effectively reached with the gospel. We need to commit ourselves to evangelism at every level; personal, church-based, inter-church, regional and national, with the clear aim of making disciples and thus adding to the Church.

Many of us felt that their call was very timely, but that insufficient time was given to develop the challenge in the rest of the Congress. This positive, biblical challenge received a muted approval in the Declaration of Intent (8) 'We repent of our lack of urgency in mission, and resolve with God's help to establish as the priority in all our churches the task of making Christ fully known.'

Perhaps our obsession with worship, ministry and Bible study has been an avoidance of the basic questions 'Do we still believe in evangelism? Are we actually seeing people being converted in our churches? If we are not seeing conversions are we asking why?'

Church Growth

Many people reacted against the declared intention of the report *Let my People Grow* to look for a positive numerical increase in the number of Christians in the nation by 1980. There is a lack of understanding of the principles of church growth as outlined in Peter Wagner's book *How Your Church Can Grow*. Some of the delegates had never heard of the teaching related to it, and it might help in the implementation of these principles if a series of regional conferences were to be launched in 1978 and a national centre for teaching the principles of 'Church Growth' established.

Mission Worldwide

The Declaration of Intent (11) states: 'We repent of the narrowness of our Christian interest and vision, and we undertake to maintain informed and active concern for the worldwide spread of the gospel, for the stewardship of the world's resources, and for the cause of welfare and justice among all men.' This strong emphasis on the 'worldwide spread of the gospel' was the result of the powerful influence of our Anglican missionary societies. They have recalled us to the priority of preaching the gospel throughout the world. Although we have also seen that England is a mission area, we must never lose sight of the need to give to, and to receive from , churches overseas. With our increasing commitments to the National Church, to the social problems, and to the unity movements, the tendency is to forget overseas mission. Men and women are still needed in many parts of the world; major missionary societies have great needs for personnel and for money. Perhaps the Declaration will challenge our churches and PCCs to put missionary commitment high on the list of our priorities. From our own inner-city church we have found great joy in being able to give more, and in closer connections with Tanzania and Chile, and we have found that the more we have given away, the more the Lord has entrusted to us in our own area. This is not the motive for giving, but a very happy result! Perhaps there could also be a more imaginative use of returned missionaries, and national Christians, to come and serve in some of our multi-racial urban areas. Some societies and individuals have begun work on such a policy, but a much more co-ordinated and detailed commitment is needed by the whole Church.

A Church for the World

After each of us has responded to the invitation of Jesus 'Come to me', we must also face up to his challenge 'Go for me'. The mission of the Church is his challenge and command to all; not an optional extra for a few enthusiasts. If we are not a missionary church in our own community, in our own nation, and in the whole world, we do not have the right to be called a church in the full biblical sense. We are to go with the full gospel to all men, using many and varied methods that we have studied, and apply them in response to the Great Commission.

Many were deeply disappointed that the Archbishop of Canterbury did not give a firm clear lead in the call to a Mission to Britain. However, he did challenge us to get involved in our own regions, and many are already doing this, but even more needs to be done. Continuous mission and evangelism by every Christian in every church would, of course, change the spiritual shape of the nation very rapidly, but it is not being done. Many believe the spiritual tide has turned, but perhaps a greater concentration on prayer and evangelism, including using some of the God-called evangelists, is also needed.

This theme of mission struck home to many and

was clearly expressed in the Statement (A.1) 'We have heard again his command to go into all the world for him. We are ashamed that too often we have allowed our churches to be refuges of comfort and safety rather than communities which equip us to meet the challenge and insecurity of mission in the contemporary world.'

Where are the Evangelicals?

From the content of the programme and the books, someone remarked, 'This is a conference of white, middle-class, well-educated people from the suburban Bible belt.' Now, this might be true of the leadership, and many of the clergy, but it was a pleasant surprise to see how many were deeply concerned for urban mission. This reflects another very significant move since Keele, and reminds us that many of the younger Evangelicals are involved in inner cities and some of our vast housing estates. The original draft virtually ignored this missionary need in our nation, and two of the afternoon specialist sessions had to be very persistent to get some of their demands included in 'Gospel and Culture'.

It is in these urban situations that we have got to stay and to work through many varied opportunities of social outreach. But we must also back up all our methods by presenting Jesus Christ as Lord by life and lip. Many ministers and leaders of traditional evangelical 'preaching stations' have been broken in spirit following years of rejection. How we need to pray, to think, and to apply the gospel challenge in the way the Lord leads us in these situations.

71

Where Shall They Live?

The fundamental key to renewal in any church situation is the home. Far too many Evangelicals do not relate their home life to their church life, living miles away from their church. Every Christian, be he minister, leader or member ought to be asking several basic questions of the Lord in prayer. (1) Lord, where do you want me to live? (2) Lord, if it is not in my parish, where do you want me to worship? (3) Lord, how do you want me to use my home for you? It is essential to find the answers to these questions before we can begin to use our homes to reach out to our neighbours. For we need to love them, care for them and seek to win them for Jesus. The Lord is calling more and more of his people to see that where they live is crucial to evangelism. The greatest challenge is to converted men and women to stay in the urban, and often rural areas. Others are being challenged to go and live in difficult areas, leaving the security of larger churches. Perhaps this vision of many Anglicans will be increasingly shared by other churches who have often retreated as denominations from these difficult areas.

Many churches with well-equipped buildings, large staff, and in the midst of settled communities may well be challenged to see whether they could provide a positive link with urban churches. They could provide prayer support, financial support, and perhaps on a limited scale man-power, as long as this was always seen to be a basic supporting role, and not a dominating of the local inner city or housing estate initiatives.

It is in these areas of multi-deprivation that the missionary challenge of our nation is most apparent today, in some cases with less than 1 per cent attending any place of worship.

Trapped by the System

The challenge to mission and evangelism will only come to the churches from leaders who are concerned for the winning of souls. The tragedy is that so many leaders get caught up in the machinery of the Church as an organisation. With problems of finance, pastoral re-organisation and staffing, most of our Evangelicals in church government have little time for direct evangelism. How many of our bishops, deans, archdeacons and other leaders have time to lead individual men and women to an experience of salvation? Indeed, many of us in the full-time ministry need to ask ourselves, 'When did I last lead somebody to Christ?' or 'When did I last even try to lead somebody to Christ?' If we are not active can we expect our people to be active in mission and evangelism? Is it not time we stopped and re-assessed our part in the structures of church life and see what our true priorities are?

One of the great advantages of the growing churches in many parts of the world is that they are working without all the 'back-up system' and obligations we have. Many things that are designed to be of pastoral help can often end up as evangelistic hindrances. Perhaps if the clergy and church leaders were prepared to pray, and fix goals of winning one, or two or five each to the Lord in the next year, there would be a spiritual revolution in our parishes. Of course, this cannot be done in a mechanical or organisational way, but through prayer and sensitivity to the Holy Spirit opportunities would come!

Indiscriminate Baptism

Having accepted the fact that we live in a missionary situation in our country, an immediate pastoral problem is that of infant baptism. An increasing number of churches are unable to continue with their practice of baptising the children of anybody who asks.

A remarkable change of thinking has taken place, so that adult baptism is now declared to be 'the theological norm, but accepts that the children of Christian parents are rightly to be included'. All of us are concerned that the whole Church still refuses to take seriously the matter of infant baptism, and the recent Synod report was not adopted. The consequences are that many parishes do not agree with the policy adopted by their neighbours, and local friction grows when parents compare notes at the local clinics and schools.

If baptism is to be seriously accepted as the mark of entrance into the body of the Church, then nobody could possibly justify the practice of baptising babies at the back of the church on a Sunday afternoon when the local church members are missing. Once the change to the main service takes place, no matter what the pressure of numbers, then the whole church is made aware of what is happening and questions and challenges are soon made. 'Why is that baby being baptised if the parents are not professing or practising Christians?' The practice of indiscriminate baptism is one of the greatest barriers to local co-operation between fellow Anglicans and between local denominations. It is wrong, and should be put right as soon as possible in every parish in the country.

74

Care for the parents enquiring is fundamental, and they should never be refused baptism for their children, in fact they should be told that we shall rejoice when the baptism takes place. We then have to take time and trouble to visit them in their home, use the lay folk of the church to share their faith with them, invite them to worship, use the Thanksgiving Service to welcome them to public worship. This should then be followed up as an integral part of the adult confirmation course or rededication for those confirmed, and subsequently converted.

Our practice will be to have two training courses a year, when all adults will be treated alike, whether parents or not. When they have attended the course, and if they have accepted Christ as Saviour, then they will be presented to the Bishop. The following Sunday morning all those who have taken this step of faith and public commitment to adult membership of the church, will have their babies baptised. In some areas this might be impractical for reasons of numbers, but I believe it is essential that we aim for the following conditions. One, or both of the parents should (a) be a committed Christian, (b) have received instruction, (c) be a confirmed member, (d) be a regular communicant at the Lord's table, (e) join the electoral roll as a sign of continuing commitment.

There should be a caring visitation and follow-up team from members of the Church Council and Sunday schools who are in full agreement with the church's policy. If parents refuse to accept such a clearly defined approach, set out in terms of love and caring for the ultimate destiny of their child and themselves, then they will have rejected their rights, and not been refused.

As many accept that adult baptism will become more and more the normal practice, as fewer and fewer parents are even requesting baptism for their children and others refuse training, then dioceses should be making provision for adult baptistries in their new church building programmes.

The Child and Holy Communion

Many are unhappy that some of the more important aspects of the Bishop of Ely's report on Christian Initiation have been dropped, and want to see them looked at again as a matter of great pastoral urgency. This is especially true of the way that confirmation is used in so many churches as a 'doorway to communion' and we would want to separate the two.

This would mean that the minimum age would probably be raised to eighteen and so this would raise immediately the question of when we should allow somebody to actually take the Holy Communion for the first time. Obviously we do not want very young children to take part, as the Bible makes it clear that we should understand what we are doing. However, there is surely a very strong case for allowing our older children and young teenagers who have a simple, but clear faith in Jesus, to partake. This would of course be only for those who have been baptised, and would raise serious pastoral problems with the children attending the church whose parents have not been converted, and the children therefore not baptised. There are as many problems raised here as in the administration of infant baptism, and a great deal more careful thinking needs to be done.

Often we expect a child to make a response to Jesus

solely because we have him for a brief period in the Sunday School each week, and perhaps in a club. A much more careful approach needs to be thought out, and more frequent visits made to the homes of children whose parents are not believers. Again, many Christians seem to be leaving the spiritual education of their children to their church, and basic teaching about the Christian family and parental obligation needs to be increased.

Maturity in the Church

The Church is not equipped for mission in our nation because we have not got a mature and equipped membership to do it. Many churches aim at bringing people to confirmation, and thus to the Lord's Table, and have no vision beyond that. With the closing of mid-week Bible study and prayer meetings in many churches, and the new emphasis on the Holy Communion as the central service on Sunday morning, the time for teaching adults grows ever less. The result is often a very immature and badly informed laity who are not able to evangelise or to grow in the grace of God. A clear programme of adult education and spiritual teaching needs to be evolved in every church with our aim that we shall become mature people, reaching to the very height of Christ's full stature (Eph. 4: 13). This of course is utterly dependent upon the grace of God the Holy Spirit at work in our lives. But when this is the central aim of the church in its preaching, its teaching, its praying and the way it is organised, then things will begin to happen. Organisation alone cannot achieve this, but we can help people to find the time and the means of deepening their personal relationship with Jesus as

Lord. Are we seeking out our members and talking to them, praying with them as well as for them, about their spiritual state? Are we looking at their time-tables to see whether they are too busy for worship, Bible study, prayer and attendance at the Lord's Supper? Are we helping or hindering the work of the Holy Spirit in their lives and in their homes?

As a minister I am often helped by Christians who have been tested by suffering. I can recall a deputy churchwarden dying of cancer, whose testimony and conversation was a great help to me. One of the effects of television on so many Christians, and others, is that we become insensitive to suffering in other parts of the world. In earlier days the mass-media had a positive teaching role through the news and current affairs programmes, making us immediately aware of great disasters and wars. But I wonder whether there is a more subtle and deeper effect, in that we can now sit back and calmly continue eating our evening meals by the side of the set that is churning out the latest disaster. Is it because we cannot cope with all the world's problems day in and day out? What is this doing to our children? Can they distinguish now between the reality of the shootings in Armagh and those in the latest 'Starsky and Hutch' programme? Are we also being sensitive to all who suffer in our own localities as we find ourselves unable to cope on a global pattern?

Reality of the Opposition

The mass-media are exploiting the increasing awareness of the forces of evil through films like *The Exorcist*, *The Omen* and many others. Far too often the Church seems strangely unaware of what is happening, and falls short of helping those in the greatest need. We need to remind ourselves of the reality of the spiritual warfare all God's people are committed to, for 'we are not fighting against human beings but against the wicked spiritual forces in the heavenly places, the rulers, authorities, the cosmic powers of this dark age' (Eph. 6: 12). All need teaching about the power of Satan and the greater power available through the Holy Spirit bringing to us the result of Christ's great victory at Calvary. Some need special help as they may be possessed by evil spirits, and we need to acknowledge the need for, and co-operate with, officially appointed diocesan exorcists, both clergy and laity. Again, many churches have been so involved in the things of this world and contemporary society, that some have almost lost the dimension of the supernatural altogether, and we need to deepen their maturity in Jesus through the Spirit.

Every Member Ministry

The greatest single factor that has inhibited mission to our nation and effective life in the local church is the emphasis on the 'one man ministry'. Centuries of emphasis on the 'ordained man' being in a unique way responsible for everything in the local church is not easily dispensed with. Yet this is essential for life, health and vitality in every parish. Every member is part of the *laos* or people of God, and every member has a ministry within the whole body of Christ.

The way this is worked out in the present situation in our country is going to be crucial for ongoing mission. The inhibiting factors will be the ways in which the law will need to be altered in the recommendations of the General Synod. The Synod is disproportionately comprised of those whose theological stance is not sympathetic to many of the Congress's beliefs and statements.

Two positions emerged at Nottingham about the precise role of the men and women who should be called to share in oversight. Some pressed for every church to evolve a lay-eldership scheme based on the New Testament pattern of a group of presbyters, or elders. These would press for them to share in the full ministry of oversight, preaching, teaching, visiting and presiding as authorised laity at the Holy Communion. Others, led by Michael Green, would argue that this is impractical at the present time, and therefore argued for a group of locally ordained men.

These two divergent ways of working have a great deal in common. Both are looking for men and women in every local church, who are spiritually mature and equipped for leadership, who should be licensed or authorised by the Bishop to work in that place and to share with a minister the oversight of that church.

This new system would do away with the present order of Readers, formerly known as Lay Readers, and would include men and women, but would always be under the leadership of a man. The emphasis in the new system must be on their spiritual vitality and maturity, and relationship to the local community. They must be trained in short courses in their home church location and must have been chosen as a result of it 'seeming good to the Holy Spirit and to us' (Acts 15: 28). The possibilities for such a ministry are tremendous and often spark off further initiatives in

80

local leadership.

In our own situation one local person was set aside as a youth leader in 1968 being paid through the generosity of one person making a very substantial covenant. From that has now emerged a situation where three members of this inner-city church are working full-time as youth and community workers in our buildings. In recent years these full-time 'unofficial staff', the rector, lady worker and the wardens have begun a shared oversight system. This has meant dividing up the congregational roll into lists. Each person is given a list every fifteen weeks and is committed to visiting everybody on it. In the home we share an agreed passage of Scripture, talk to and pray with each one. As the congregation has grown substantially over the past two years we are now including seven others who are acknowledged to have spiritual gifts by the church. They too will share the oversight and encourage other people to use their gifts in turn for the benefit of the church and the community we serve. Four others will visit everybody in the area having a baby, to talk to them about the opportunities of the Thanksgiving Service, playgroups, Sunday Schools, Family Service and related organisations. Another team of four, sensitive older people, is being used in visiting the bereaved as follow-up after funerals.

It is as we look at the organisational, administrative life of our church that we find the 'one-man-band' concept dies hardest. Why does the vicar hang on to the chairing of the Parochial Church Council, the finance committee, or the building committee, when often there are far more competent people in the church council? It is only as we are seen to be trusting our own people and releasing the reins of power, that others in the church will be willing to do the same. One of the greatest needs of our churches, of all denominations, is for the discerning, developing, and use of every member's gifts. It is as people are released to do the job that the Lord is calling them to that the way forward in mission and evangelism will become possible.

The main problem at local level is to break out of the vicious circle that traps churches. The minister often longs to use people, but they need training, and he is often needed to train them. But to train them he needs time and release from many jobs that he shouldn't be doing. To be released he must appoint others, but they need training. So it appears, until after prayer and wide consultation with the whole church the decisive step forward is taken. Of course there will be misunderstanding; for example when one of the congregation visits and is greeted with 'It's not you I want, I want to see the vicar'. But after a short time trust develops and the obvious spiritual benefits to the whole church decisively prove the case.

Use of Other Gifts

In addition to oversight, there is a tremendous need to develop other gifts of the Spirit (1 Cor. 12–14, and Eph. 4). Obviously there will be differing interpretations about some of the more specific gifts between those involved in the charismatic movement and others. But there is an enormous amount of common ground that should not be overlooked. The churches that recognise the use of the gifts of the Spirit around the world are growing fastest in number and maturity.

The use of gifts is a tremendously vital one if we want our churches to advance in terms of mission.

Regional colleges, perhaps integrated with some of the teachers' training colleges, would also be of vital strategic importance in training the laity for ministry.

The Place of Women in Ministry

Little has been said recently about the role of women in ministry, perhaps because so many now accept that they have a full and rightful place within it. A consensus view seems to be emerging that women should be ordained, both as full-time paid ministers and as local presbyters. However, many add the rider that in developing group leadership the final responsibility will be with an individual male as president of the group. But more and more use should be made of our ladies in developing their gifts in music, movement, drama, visiting and full oversight of the churches.

The Role of Bishops

As we re-examine the role of the local clergy, so we must also see what we expect of our diocesan bishops. The bishop is the visible link between the individual churches in an area. He should be enabled to provide spiritual oversight, or *episcope*, and not to be trapped by the system into being primarily an administrator. The introduction of Synodical Government has meant that our bishops now are enabled to share their oversight 'in council' with their clergy and laity. But often the size of the dioceses has meant the bishops being remote from both clergy and people. It is interesting to note that Salisbury now has a dozen retired bishops and archbishops helping the diocesan staff. Some of the northern dioceses have none, and so perhaps the call needs to be uttered 'come north, older men and help us!' It used to be ordinands and curates who were rebuked for the southern drift, but perhaps our 'fathers in God' will respond to the challenge and set an example to us all.

One of the major reasons for the failure of the parish churches to be stimulated into effective action, meaningful worship, and spiritual attractiveness is the minister at the centre. Many men have been worn out by the pressures of the system, others have lost their joy and vitality and seem to see the future in terms of failure. They are content to run their parishes facing diminishing numbers with the same attitude as the band on the bridge of the *Titanic*, gradually sinking beneath the waves. Our bishops need to make the visitation, spiritual counsel, or replacement of such men a matter of the very greatest urgency.

Patterns of Growth

One of the contemporary tragedies of church life is the rejection of so many of the denominational structures and churches. This has led to the rapid growth of the house-church movement amongst both charismatic and non-charismatic Evangelicals. For so many of their leaders this is a result of earlier conversion and commitment in universities, or colleges, or assemblies where great emphasis has been placed upon the individual and his commitment to Christ. But often this has led to too little emphasis upon the whole doctrine of the Church, and of consequent commitment to it. A great responsibility now falls on those involved in the leadership of Christian Unions to ensure that this type of teaching about individual response to Jesus Christ as Saviour is balanced by teaching and practice of commitment to his church. It is as Christians see their need for each other's ministries, and common life in worship, evangelism, teaching and mission that the church will grow in a locality.

Within each congregation our structures often prevent us effectively being the church of Christ in deepest fellowship. We need to re-examine our structures and see just what we are doing with our timetables and our particular style of worship, to build, or destroy real fellowship. One thing we did some years ago was to abolish the early morning communion service, and to ensure that the Holy Communion was an integral part of the main services. This is done by having it within the morning or evening worship alternate weeks, and has at least ensured that we have only two groups to try to integrate. How can this be done?

First we must discern what groups are identifiable within the present structure, and see how these can be best related to each other. For instance, we let the Youth group fetch the elderly folk once a month and give them a guest tea. They are joined there by students, younger widows or lonely people and all have the meal together. They then go on into the monthly Guest Service conducted by a special group each month. Over the course of the year this means that all the main groups relate to the whole congregation and to the guests.

Another major factor is the use of 'all-age' fellowship meals, outings, and holidays. On our Anniversary Sunday 120 people had lunch together after the

Family Service, an outing including organised games, then tea, and closed with a special Guest Service. Nearly one hundred of us will enjoy two weeks away together this summer on the parish holiday. All these activities are intended to draw us closer together for united worship, encouragement, teaching and sharing the gifts of the many rather than the few.

In examining the structures one of the most painful jobs will be deciding what parts of the time-table are in effect removing folk from the opportunities of contacting their neighbours. Over-structured and over-organised churches are often least capable of sustaining evangelism and mission if they simply use those meetings for 'escape'. Tensions arose at the Congress on this subject, however, because there is often a different way of working in rural, urban and suburban settings, and we have to be sensitive to establish what is right in our own community. In our own inner-city situation we have found that bridge-building opportunities have come most often through playgroups, pensioners' lunch clubs, keep-fit classes and open clubs. The house groups have been most effective for fellowship and teaching rather than evangelism, but the opposite was obviously the case in many of the suburban churches represented at Nottingham.

Training the Full-Time Paid Clergy

A dual crisis is looming in the present system of training men. The first is financial as most of the local authorities have cancelled second training grants, and also many university fees are climbing because of inflation. The second is that of falling numbers, mainly because the role of the clergyman and the nature of ordination appear so confused to many of the young men in our churches.

We still need to pray for young men, called out from, and sent by the parishes to be trained in theological colleges. Serious questions about the present training will need to be asked, and what type of ministry men are being called to. Men need to be prepared now for when the new local eldership or presbyter systems are developed in the whole Church. Far greater emphasis on training men and women to work in team and group ministries, as well as within parish church teams, is needed. Perhaps one of the colleges could be visionary enough to found a Department of Urban Mission and Evangelism. This is desperately needed in our national life as more and more Evangelicals are responding to the challenge of the inner cities, the pre-war large housing estates and some of the great problems of the post-war high-rise flat situations. There are training courses, but all working on a voluntary basis, and surely the time has come for the whole Church to commit itself in a far more serious way to this challenge of urban deprivation. There is of course an equally valid case for another college to found a department of Rural Mission and Evangelism to help people who will be called to minister in situations of rapid rural depopulation. Such departments in the colleges could be used for 'in-service' training for many men who need to research and co-ordinate what is already happening in many exciting situations.

These colleges could also be the regional service centres for the Theological Training by Extension for all the local elders or presbyters, as is happening in so many parts of the world. It is certainly hoped that the new plans for dispersing the colleges will not end up in dispensing with the distinctive and differing traditions of training. The greatest error would be to end up with dreary monotony in 'central and safe' colleges where Evangelical and Anglo-Catholic teaching have been squeezed out. Most of us are so grateful for the richness and variety in our national Church and would resist all efforts to deprive us of them.

Series 3 Services

The fact that these services, when revised, will probably be the basis for a new Prayer Book in 1980 was obviously in the minds of the delegates. The various services had a mixed reception, with infant baptism needing clarifying and clearer teaching about the need for conversion. But welcome was given to the emphasis on joy, freedom, flexibility and congregational involvement. Far from reverting to the ministerial monologues greater lay involvement was called for. Many new forms of worship are being experimented with in drama, mime, dance, music, movement and spiritual gifts. Some of the delegates at Morecambe in 1972 were amazed at the newer forms of worship used there by Anglicans. If they had been at Nottingham and seen the dancing and drama they would have been speechless! More and more churches, charismatic and non-charismatic, are involving more and more members with their spiritual gifts to build each other up.

The Series 3 Communion was viewed with concern, as some cannot use it in its present form, but further possible revision would probably make it acceptable to most. Congress therefore is calling for re-examination of 'petition for the dead, eucharistic sacrifice or reservation of the sacraments'. It is also hoped that the Prayer of Thanksgiving (formerly called the Consecration Prayer) will focus much more clearly and specifically on the death of Christ. This is the main part of the service and we all need clear reminding of the great fact of the true and perfect sacrifice made once and for all for us on Calvary.

Charismatic Evangelicals

At the Keele Congress in 1967 the whole subject of the influence of the charismatic renewal movement was hardly mentioned. Things have moved a long way since then, and the whole area of relationships was looked at in a helpful and positive way. This had been helped by the publication of the *Gospel and Spirit* joint statement prepared and agreed by a group nominated by the Fountain Trust and the Church of England Evangelical Council. Well-known charismatic leaders like Michael Harper, Harold Parks, Tom Smail, Tom Walker and David Watson have been involved. During the last decade much damage has been done by divisions and disharmony in many churches as a result of arrogant assertions by 'charismatics' or ill-informed rejection by 'non-charismatics'. Congress managed to debate many of the subjects connected with 'charismatic' ministry and worship in a spirit of love and understanding. Clear acknowledgment of the influence of the renewal movement on the Church of Rome was given, and the fact that many 'non-charismatic' churches were using spiritual gifts.

One point of disagreement however was that concerning the place of modern prophecy. Many seriously doubted whether prophecy is a genuine gift from God for the churches today. They would argue from Ephesians 2: 20 that apostles and prophets were primary, or foundational, gifts for the Church in New Testament days. Once the Scriptures were completed there was no further need for them as the Bible is now our primary source of the revelation of God. Some would argue that God the Holy Spirit still gives to some the sense of speaking a direct word from the Lord to the church. It was agreed, however, that there should be clear safeguards provided in these cases.

(1) The message of the prophets must always be tested by the Bible and if the message is not in agreement with Scripture then it must be rejected as false.

(2) The lives of the prophets must be tested also, and the church must only be willing to listen to prophets of spiritual maturity and integrity. An adverse example is David Berg (Moses of the Children of God) who clearly lives an immoral life and contradicts Scripture by his 'revelations'.

(3) Their messages are related to individual local situations and are not to be taken as modern additions to Scripture.

These safeguards were proposed by John Stott and found general acceptance. The points are taken up in 'Christian Maturing' where 'the widespread emphasis on spiritual gifts in the contemporary church' are welcomed, whilst recognising that discernment is necessary concerning their validity, and patience concerning their use. 'We believe they have an important part to play, together with other gifts, in the bringing of the Church to full maturity in Christ (H.7).'

The Unity Statement (L.5) also saw that the renewal movement had been helpful in drawing people back to God in putting him first and denominations second. Some still had very large question marks over some of the teaching and expressions associated with the charismatic movement. However, the main concern expressed by Congress was that we should now seek to live and work together in a constructive and not divisive way.

This will be a challenge to many of the newly formed 'house churches', created by the charismatic renewal movement, to reconsider their position. Many would feel that they are not proceeding in the best way and should be re-integrated into local mainline denominational churches.

The Caring Church

One of the most positive and helpful challenges to the Congress is the call to us to re-examine the membership of our local congregation. We have already thought of the structures as helps or hindrances to growth, but we also need to think of the individuals within them. It is only as the individuals within the church grow in grace and maturity that evangelism will be seen as an essential part of the life of the church.

Oliver O'Donovan in 'Marriage and the Family', has challenged us to see whether we are supporting or destroying Christian family life. Sometimes our leaders spend so much time in active Christian service outside the home that they fail as parents, or even as partners. We need to 're-emphasise the joyful and fulfilling nature of parenthood, and to offer greater help and guidance to parents in the upbringing of their children'. We are very concerned that many Christians are now being divorced, or separated, and much more teaching and counselling is needed.

All congregations have single people in them and we need to accept that for some time this is a calling from God and not a mark of failure. Yet we must also be sensitive to those who long to be married, and feel depressed or frustrated because they are not. In addition to these there are all the older widows, widowers, those left after divorce, and one-parent families. All these belong to the family of Christ and need caring for, so that they can contribute to, and benefit by, the life of the fellowship. Whatever our view of divorce, each person is one who needs especial love, care and understanding by the whole church and not just by the minister and leaders.

Every effort must be made to see that every member is cared for, visited, and prayed for and seen as of supreme importance to the Lord and to his church.

One of the more controversial sections (B.3) dealt with the care of homosexuals. Most Christians, and many churches, are not very well informed on the subject and find it very difficult to distinguish between homosexual nature and homosexual acts. All of us would denounce any homosexual act as being contrary to the Word of God, but realise that there are Christians who are homosexual by nature. These individuals need special pastoral care and support and a welcome within the fellowship of the church. Any feeling of rejection by the fellowship will make it especially hard for them and may very easily drive them to commit acts that could otherwise have been prevented. A great deal more thought needs to be given to this subject of care for the individual, and to teaching the whole congregation about pastoral care.

Prospects for Unity

John Stott has called us to gladly recognise as our Christian brothers and sisters all those who from the heart confess Jesus as Lord, whether or not they wear an evangelical label, and even if they do not hold as full a biblical faith as we say they should. There are many such in the historic denominations, but how far should we go in seeking formal unity with them?

The Declaration of Intent (6) states 'We reaffirm our commitment to the goal of visible unity in Christ's Church, and declare our conviction that the starting point of visible unity is a common confession of faith in Christ leading on to the fellowship of congregations at the Lord's table.'

In the past many Evangelicals have been content to take part in Keswick Conventions or a Billy Graham Crusade, and experience effective unity of purpose and action. After the convention or crusade is over, we have gone home to continue to worship in our separate churches and chapels. Is this good enough? And if not, what can be done about it? In theory the major denominations are working towards eventual unity on the basis of the Ten Propositions. However, it is quite obvious that there is very little desire for unity in the parishes of our nation, or indeed even in the General Synod.

Balanced against a commitment in principle must

be the fears of many ordinary Christians in becoming involved in a great monochrome organisational structure. We must admit that there are so many problems in the present denominations, that putting them all together is not a very happy thought. If the individual denominations are not faithful to the Word of God, open to the Spirit, and being renewed for mission and evangelism, they are hardly likely to become so by an Act of Unity.

Now this is not a popular view, but it is a realistic one. We have often lost our sense of direction and purpose, and perhaps Nottingham will make us reassess our priorities in terms of spiritual unity or organisational unity.

We will all have to make special efforts to keep in close contact with FIEC and similar independent churches. In many of our urban areas the most rapidly growing churches are the so-called 'black churches' and again we must keep contact and deepen fellowship with them.

Ten Propositions

The Propositions are being debated by eight denominations and are not a programme for union, but only a modest step on the way. They are inviting the churches to recognise each other's ministers and members as true members of the body of Christ, and to try to bring closer fellowship between denominations. The Church of England is approaching them in its usual ponderous way, and after several debates at the General Synod has now referred them to the Diocesan Synods for a reply to the basic motion 'That the Diocesan Synod shares the view of the General

Synod that the Ten Propositions of the Churches' Unity Commission provide an acceptable basis for continued consultation with the other Churches which are our partners in the Commission.'

The Roman Catholic Church has already published a provisional reply, showing that the Ecumenical Commission is unable to accept Propositions 4, 5 and 6, and cannot recommend action on 2. It commends action by others who are able to proceed further.

This has led us 'to fear that the actual progress they offer towards visible unity may be so slow that consideration of them may be overtaken by boredom'. Congress is therefore urging that we do not wait until all protracted negotiations are completed but to get on with what we can locally. Far-reaching proposals about sharing of buildings and the pooling of financial and pastoral resources at local level and in larger diocesan and denominational areas have been made.

Perhaps it is as well that practical steps are being taken, because we are all aware of great problems raised in the Propositions, and especially (6). It would seem impossible at this stage for a 'complete agreement to be reached within the Church of England on the meaning of "we recognise . . . the ordained ministers of other churches" '. If there were any attempt to bring forward a Service of Recognition that involved the 'laying on of episcopal hands' there would be a vigorous reaction in our Church. Congress spelt this out in detail so that there would be no repetition of the Anglican–Methodist fiasco. We, as Evangelicals, accept that the ministers of all other denominations are 'ordained ministers' in the fullest sense. This is because we value episcopacy, but do not accept that it is essential for the existence of the Church, and indeed ought to be reformed within our own church.

There are, of course, other problems about the nature of 'the covenant', how Baptists could possibly accept infant baptism, or Paedo-Baptists accept that Baptists re-baptise their members. The next ten years or so will see an incredible number of hours spent debating at different levels of church life—pray God that at least some of it will prove to be worth while at the end of the day.

The Numbers Game

In the Unity section consideration is given to the attitudes of participating churches when unity is discussed. Some churches have steadily declined since the war and consequently feel under great pressure. When the Anglican-Methodist talks were being held it was obvious that many saw the proposed Union rather as a 'take-over'. This was because there are nearly two million adult members of the Church of England as against just over half a million Methodists. But in world unity schemes the picture is rather different with about sixty-five million Anglicans and seventy million Methodists. This fact obviously colours talks on ARCIC too as in this country there are approximately equal numbers of committed Anglicans and Roman Catholics, but twenty-seven million baptised Anglicans as against only four million Roman Catholics. In the world figures there is a tremendous difference: there are six hundred million Roman Catholics as against sixty-five million members of the Anglican Communion.

The various churches taking part in the Ten Propositions debate vary tremendously in size and perhaps it is worth noting this. The first figure given is that for adult membership and the second is for all members including children. Baptist Union 148,889; 450,000. Churches of Christ 3,500; 10,000. The Church of England 1,985,703; 27,000,000 (baptised). Congregational Federation 9,104; 28,000. Methodist Church 526,548; 1,429,103. Moravian Church 4,484; 14,000. The Roman Catholics 1,790,980; 4,182,209. The United Reformed Church 169,182; 500,000. These figures are all taken from the booklet *Visible Unity in Life and Mission* published by the Church Information Office as a background discussion paper to the Ten Propositions.

Relationships with Rome

After the Keele Congress in 1967 many of our friends in the Free Churches thought we were no longer interested in them. This was due to the new emphasis and commitment of Anglican Evangelicals to stay in the Church of England. Some of us fear that following Nottingham 1977 the rift may widen, as we have spent so much time talking about our attitude to, and relationships with, the Roman Catholics.

The Declaration of Intent sought to balance this by stating, 'In grief we find ourselves at a distance from our evangelical brothers in other denominations, we undertake to seek closer fellowship and co-operation with them in informal consultation, in shared worship, and in united outreach.' The Declaration is not nearly as specific as the Group Statement (6) 'seeing ourselves and Roman Catholics as fellow-Christians, we repent of attitudes that seem to deny it.' Declaration 7 states 'Deeply regretting past attitudes of indifference and ill-will towards Roman Catholics, we renew our commitment to seek with them the truth of God and the unity he wills, in obedience to our common Lord on the basis of Scripture.'

Many Evangelicals in all churches would agree with the Declaration and are seeking to share the Bible and to talk with Roman Catholics. But for many the basic problem remains. 'What is a Christian?' Nowhere in our statements do we face the basic concept of the new birth or conversion, or the reality of spiritual experience, which has united Evangelicals of all persuasions in the past.

Obviously attitudes have changed since Vatican II and the charismatic renewal movement came into being in the Church of Rome. But fundamental doctrines have not changed and cannot change. Some are hoping and praying for a new reformation from within the Church of Rome, but history shows that this is a virtual impossibility by the very nature of the system.

A distinct division emerged as we thought of the historic fact of the Reformation. Both Julian Charley and David Watson referred to the Reformation as a tragedy and drew widespread protests from delegates. Most of us would say that it was a means of great blessing to the Church with a single tragic side, that of division. To give the impression that the tragic side was of more importance than the stand for the truth is a great sadness. For many of us the Reformation was the greatest revival in history and we have our present spiritual liberty as a direct result from it.

We accept that many barriers have been broken down and discussions are taking place, but we are concerned about the dangers inherent in this. The

Church of Rome has got to make great doctrinal changes before we can even think that there is real hope on the horizon for union. As the CEEC/Fountain Trust joint statement on *Gospel and Spirit* reminds us: (1) A unity based on experience at the expense of doctrine would be less than the unity envisaged in the New Testament and would be dangerous in the long term. (2) Personal (and even corporate) renewal has not always meant the dropping of all anti-biblical or sub-biblical traditions and practices. We see the need to pray for, and to encourage reformation by God's Word as well as renewal by his Spirit in all churches.

The present three Statements on the Eucharist, the Ministry, and Tradition published by the Anglican and Roman Catholic International Commission certainly do not look very promising to Evangelicals. In fact it would appear that Evangelicals in the Church of England may well have to fight their battles all over again, as was predicted by Bishop Ryle. We cannot ignore the change taking place in both our churches, but we can insist that everything is subject to the supreme authority of Scripture.

However, many of us would admit that we must be better informed about Rome and her new emphases. There are so many contradictory statements from 'conservatives' and 'radicals'. We would need to see major changes in position with regard to Scripture as the final authority. All traditions and official statements made by Councils and by Popes must be subject to Scripture. The anathemas pronounced at the Council of Trent would need to be revoked. All teaching about Christ being sacrificed afresh in the Mass would also need to be revoked, but the unique nature of the cross must be re-affirmed. Much teaching about the Virgin Mary, her immaculate conception, bodily assumption and role in redemption and prayer would need changing. But the fundamental change needed is that concerning 'Justification by Grace through Faith'. Oh, how we long to see Christ so preached that men and women in many more Anglican and Roman Catholic churches might know the assurance of sins forgiven.

Non-Anglican Evangelicals

Immediately we seek to draw closer to Rome we must realise that our links with non-Anglican Evangelicals will become much more difficult. Denominations will welcome such overtures, but within these, the evangelical groups will find the future more difficult. We have traditionally had close ties with fellow-believers, born again by the Spirit and 'All one in Christ Jesus' as the Keswick motto says. Have we as Anglican Evangelicals been too hasty in our approaches? Must we not look again at our deepest relationships with our 'evangelical brothers in Christ'? Is there not a real need to spend time together in such activities as Keswick, the Evangelical Alliance and related Tear Fund, and the Scripture Union? Surely the challenge of the Declaration of Intent (4) must be taken as a matter of priority: 'In grief that we find ourselves at a distance from our evangelical brothers in other denominations, we undertake to seek closer fellowship and co-operation with them in informal consultation, in shared worship, and in united outreach.'

How far are we Anglicans aware of what is happening in other circles? There is the growth of the

Methodist Revival Fellowship and other evangelical growth in Methodism especially in the colleges. There is the Group for Evangelism and Renewal in the United Reformed Church. The Baptist Church colleges have many more Evangelicals in them, and this is true of the independent Bible colleges also. The Elim Pentecostal Church is showing remarkable progress in church growth and expansion, buying up many redundant churches. Its college at Capel is full, and again students are at many Bible colleges which all seem to be full. This cannot all be ascribed to the charismatic renewal as so many of the new house churches, evangelists, and Bible college students have not been involved in it.

At the 'Strategy for Evangelism' conference at Morecambe, David Pawson commented that the spiritual tide had turned, and was coming in. Perhaps it has done so a little more slowly than he expected, but all the evidence points to the fact that things are happening in our nation. It would be a great tragedy if, at such a time as this, the gap widened between evangelicals.

We Anglicans have to accept that many FIEC churches cannot understand our position as Evangelicals within a comprehensive church. They want to deal with us in terms of exclusiveness and feel that we are not interested in them if we seek to talk to non-Evangelicals in our own church as well as to them.

Another great problem is that since our commitment to the new life-style of our churches, to our denomination, and to so many other factors in community life, we are simply running out of time! We seem to be run off our feet and haven't the time to fraternise with our evangelical friends outside our own denomination. Free Churches don't have all the complicated machinery of parish, deanery, archdeaconry, and diocese, and have much more time to sit and talk and pray in fellowship. When we plead 'we are too busy' they often feel rejected.

Perhaps we need to take much more time to examine our local structures and see what we can do to promote closer understanding. We need to be constantly inviting our Free Church friends to our Communion services, Bible studies and fellowship meetings.

If we committed ourselves to a regional policy of 'Mission and Evangelism', a programme of united action and outreach would draw us closer together. Joint evangelism brings a sense of close relationship quicker than anything else. It is at such times that our 'unity in the Spirit' becomes of much more importance than 'long-term organisational unity'. Both have their place, but mission gives us a vision of the reality of what we can and should do together in planning, prayer and evangelism.

Which Unity Do We Want?

The great problem for those of us in parish work is to find the right way forward in the search for unity. Basic principles would lead us to work for 'one church in one place' and this would consequently lead us to support the ecumenical movement. But, as we examine the workings of the whole unity movement, we see very little evidence of the Holy Spirit at work in it. On the other hand, we can, and do, find deep spiritual relationships with brethren in our local churches, and find joy and power in fellowship, worship, prayer and united evangelism. We agree about so much that is basic in our attitude to the Scriptures, to Jesus Christ and salvation, that united action is easier. The Archbishop of Canterbury and the Pope urged us to work at evangelism together—but what agreed gospel would we preach, and how would we tell people they can find salvation? Perhaps there is a lot more talking to do before such action is really effective, or we might well find that expediency in action would be taking the place of foundational doctrines. There are far more Evangelicals in all denominations wanting fellowship and action first, and unity talks second, than perhaps our leaders realise.

I personally feel these pressures very much. On the one hand there is the tension of how to deepen the existing fellowship with those who are my 'brothers in Christ' but who belong to other groups, denominations or mission halls. Then there is the scriptural call to be united with ALL in the local area to be 'the church in each place' but often there is so little agreement about doctrine, life or structures. Then there is the post-Keele challenge to be more involved in the Church of England—and no matter how much this is done at administrative levels, what real fellowship can one have with radicals? We often exist at a superficial level in the deanery because we never dig down deep enough to find what really matters to us. As long as we keep away from discussion about what evangelism, mission, the new birth, conversion and commitment mean, we can survive together. But is that enough? I leave you to face that challenge in your own heart.

What Shall We Do First?

One of the problems of churches in the post-NEAC era will be in deciding what is the right thing to do in our situation. There is such a diversity of composition, location, size, spirituality that the very greatest sensitivity is needed. For example, in the area of music and hymns which are so crucial in worship and evangelism, what should we do in our churches? The contrast between the great orchestra of All Souls leading two thousand people singing from *Sound of Living Waters*, and a five-voice choir accompanied by a worn-out organ can be devastating. We hear the calls to experiment with drama, mime, dance, interview techniques, more audio-visual aids involving the people. Then we hear calls to start training the laity for pastoral visitation, preaching, teaching, being involved in local politics and community life. From another group comes the call to develop 'house groups' or 'all-age study schools', from another group 'get involved in local radio, write for the newspapers'. Another group says get involved as managers in local schools, or train as marriage guidance councillors. If we sit and read the whole statement and try to respond to everything at once, we could do great damage to the spiritual life of our congregation.

All of these crucial matters need our attention, but we have to determine under God what our own church is capable of at this stage of its spiritual growth. We need to get the council together and assess our present programme to see what should be retained or removed. We should be prepared to identify our present strengths and see how they can be developed. We should also acknowledge our weaknesses and see how they can be rectified. We then need to discern the gifts of the Spirit within our congregation and pray and encourage people to use them. We need to set attainable goals for the next year, and for the long term, in every area of life, and seek the people and the right methods of fulfilling them. This is the visionary style leadership that our churches need if they are to respond adequately to the Declaration of Intent (12) 'We admit that we have often tolerated low standards in our worship, and apathy in our spiritual life, and we pledge ourselves by prayer and action to seek renewal in our local churches.'

Encouraged to go Forward

We need encouragement to go forward in this country by the growth of the church in the world. As the Bishop of Winchester has reminded us, 'Mission is no longer from here to there or there to here, but to everywhere to everywhere else.' I am indebted to Canon Harry Sutton for many of the thoughts that he shared with us as a result of his recent world tour studying growth points in the Church in many continents. In the UK only 6 per cent of the population attend any place of worship on a Sunday, and in many inner-city areas less than 1 per cent. How do we reach the 94 per cent and how do we solve the problem that so few of the 6 per cent who do attend seem to care about evangelism and mission? It is because so many churches spend so much time with the 6 per cent and have no vision for the 94 per cent that many house churches have sprung up independent of us?

But look away from secular, materialistic Western

Europe and what do we see? In Africa there were 20 million Christians in 1950; 90 million by 1970, 130 million by 1977 and at the present rate of growth there will be 395 million by the year 2000: that is, more on that continent than any other in the world, but would we gather that from the media? Dr David Barrett of Nairobi says, 'The most massive influx into the Church in the whole of history is taking place at this time on the continent of Africa.' We find in our own church having a positive link with the Church in Tanzania a great stimulation and encouragement.

We could repeat the picture of growth in Indonesia of half a million in 1910 to 6 million in 1975 with many Muslims being converted. In South Korea there is a mighty out-pouring of the Holy Spirit with 15 per cent converted people and 50 per cent attending a place of worship every Sunday. In Latin America the Church is growing three times faster than the birth rate, in general terms. In 1910 there were not more than 100,000 Protestants in the whole of Latin America, and now there are 20 million and a growth rate of 10 per cent each year. In the USA and Canada similar exciting growth is taking place in many areas, and these facts should all combine to remind us that God the Holy Spirit is very much at work in the world for which Christ died. In all these places growth is not just in numbers, but praise God is also in spiritual maturity and life. But how some of us who are used to 50–100 each Sunday would cope with the 25,000 in a San Paulo church is worth thinking about!

There are various factors in these situations that do not apply, but there are some that should encourage us as we seek to find the way forward in Britain.

(1) *The Church will only grow where the members*

want it to grow. Here we need to challenge our commitment to evangelism, and seek to implement our Declaration at Nottingham. Resolutions at congresses and Church Councils will not do it, but individuals and churches that are seeking the leading of the Spirit can.

(2) *Clear Goals*—knowing what we are going to do about tomorrow. Here the principles of *Let my People Grow* need to be closely spelt out in the local church.

(3) *Methods that work.* In Africa they have developed 'New Life for All' in South America 'Evangelism in Depth', and in South Korea, 'National Evangelistic Campaign'. The common factor is that they are using a method that works for them, in their situation. At the Congress we heard of people using 'Evangelism Explosion', and from Bryan Gilbert about 'One Step Forward', and in the Urban Mission sessions we discovered varied approaches in many different cities. Each church must seek to find just what is the right method for them, whether house groups, personal visitation, social activities or some other.

(4) *Membership is mobilised.* In South America the clue to the growth of a church is 'in direct proportion to its ability to mobilise its total resources in the continuous declaration of what it believes to be true'. In the inner cities the most effective evangelism is done by the individual members of the church being able to share with their neighbours about the Saviour and what he means to them. We have found that this can be done with young mums at a keep fit class or with the pensioners at a lunch club or in the playgroup. It has come about through the deepening friendships in the house groups and as a follow-up to

baptism and funeral visits.

(5) *Leadership*. All the churches that are growing are those with visionary leadership; what Peter Wagner calls 'possibility thinkers', and not like so many clergy and lay leaders, 'impossibility thinkers'. Are we overwhelmed by the size of the task, the number in the parish, the apathy of the congregation, or the problems of antiquated buildings? Dare we begin to see what hidden resources there are in the congregation, in what ways we can adapt buildings, and how the Lord can transform the most difficult situation into a glorious opportunity? This sort of vision should be shared with as many of the local leaders as possible, as it is surely here that 'enthusiasm is caught as well as taught'.

(6) *Use of Evangelists*. Expert research has shown that about 10 per cent of each congregation have been given the 'gift of evangelist' by the Holy Spirit. Peter Wagner comments that very few people are really using the gift, but where they are, the church is growing.

Christ Not Christianity

Often our churches are obstacles to people finding faith in Christ. We need to be very clear about the nature and content of our evangelism. The Lausanne Covenent paragraph (4) challenges us as to the nature of evangelism: 'To evangelise is to spread the good news that Jesus Christ died for our sins and was raised from the dead according to the Scriptures, and that as the reigning Lord he now offers the forgiveness of sins and the liberating gift of the Spirit to all who repent and believe. Our Christian presence in the world is

108

indispensable to evangelism, and so is that kind of dialogue whose purpose is to listen sensitively in order to understand. But evangelism itself is the proclamation of the historical, biblical Christ as Saviour and Lord, with a view to persuading people to come to him personally and so be reconciled to God. In issuing the gospel invitation we have no liberty to conceal the cost of discipleship. Jesus still calls all who would follow him to deny themselves, take up their cross, and identify themselves with his new community. The results of evangelism include obedience to Christ, incorporation into his Church and responsible service in the world.'

Jim Packer forcefully reminded us of the way that the person of Jesus is often watered down in modern theology. Indeed a special congress resolution called on the Archbishops 'publicly to confirm that the Church of England still stands by its historic faith in the Christ of the Scriptures and the Creeds'. We were challenged with the many faiths now present in our multi-racial society, especially in urban areas, and we are committed to presenting 'Jesus the only Saviour'. We must use every possible means to point people to the 'historical, biblical Christ as Saviour and Lord'. As we depend on the Spirit and challenge people to full discipleship we shall see blessing in our own lives, in our churches and the nation. This is not evangelical triumphalism but biblical realism as God honours the proclamation of the living Lord Jesus.

The Archbishop of York in the opening address told us, 'We need a new spirit of adventurous evangelism. We need a new generation of militants who will seize the opportunities that are available to us.' Dare we hope that after Nottingham we will help to raise such a new generation in the parish churches of our nation?

National Assembly on Evangelism

Immediately after the Congress the first practical steps were taken in seeking to co-ordinate national efforts in evangelism. The major denominations, the Evangelical Alliance, the Church of England Evangelical Council, the Billy Graham Evangelical Association and an observer from the Roman Catholic Church have called on Churches and Christian organisations to (1) Start immediately in reporting and evaluating evangelistic efforts of many kinds now being undertaken. (2) Plan new local initiatives in evangelism arising out of local reconciliation. (3) Explore the convergence in understanding of both message and methods.

The group proposes to call a National Assembly of Evangelicals not later than 1980 to gather the first results of this call and to assist British Christians in growing together to fulfil the common task of bringing the gospel to this nation. The invitation seeks replies to 'Are you ready to co-operate in the initiative as outlined? Would you be ready to share in the proposed National Assembly?' Surely all those who made the Declaration of Intent at Nottingham will be praying and working to see that there is much more than just a National Assembly, but positive action in the regions. 1980 will be a very significant year for us in Liverpool as we celebrate the centenary of the diocese and the city of Liverpool. Perhaps it would be appropriate for the diocese founded by Bishop J. C. Ryle to play host to the National Assembly?

Part of the discussions on evangelism hinged on the fact that a number of people want Billy Graham to return for another Crusade in this country before his retirement. Some of the delegates flew to Amsterdam to see him the day after the Congress and negotiations are still continuing. Although we are grateful for so many British evangelists and local crusades, it is still a fact that Billy Graham is the only 'name' that communicates to many people in this country. Although many of us would prefer not to have so many American 'side-shows' we would still say, 'Billy come back'. There are still many people who will respond to the big event, perhaps in their region, and it can be contained within 'organising mission' programmes. Let us not be deterred by denominational leaders who are often remote from the realities of daily evangelism and mission. The Archbishop has conceded that 'the day of big meetings is not wholly over', so let us see what could happen in regional crusades. Harringay and Earl's Court resulted in thousands being converted, and hundreds going forward to serve the Lord in 'Mission and Ministry' at home and overseas. Have we seen anything like that in 'Call to the North'?

FACING THE WORLD
Dick Williams

The Changing World

Evangelicals are 'people of the Book'. They are those
who, in John Stott's Congress assurances, 'submit to
the authority of Scripture'. But a third of their time at
the Congress was devoted to talking about social and
political matters. So for Evangelicals one question
looms large. 'What is the connection between the
Bible and matters of this kind?'

It is not unknown for some Evangelicals to say that
the Church's job is to get on with preaching the gospel
and building up the fellowship of those who respond
to it, and to let the world look after its own affairs.
There are others who say that Christianity is an
intensely personal affair, so private to its practitioners
that it has nothing to do with any one else. More
fashionably, in some circles today, there is the view
that the world is so far gone in sin that the Church's
job is to create local forms of an alternative society
withdrawn as far as possible from the larger society
which provides their members with water, drains,
electricity, medical care, police protection, and so on.

None of these notions of what the Church is, and
does, can stand up to the full impact of the Bible. For

Christians are members of the body of Christ, and Christ loved and served mankind, and told his disciples 'I am among you as one that serves'. Clearly his body must be among the nations of the world as one that serves. 'As the Father sent me', he said (John 20: 21), 'so I send you'.

The 'new commandment' which Christ gives to his followers is that we should love as he loves us. That love took him to the cross. We dazedly acknowledge the implication of that for us. Sometimes our slender grasp of what it means errupts into gale force as we sing 'When I survey the wond'rous cross . . . ' But on the way to the cross Jesus announced good news to the poor, proclaimed release for prisoners and recovery of sight for the blind, let the 'broken victims go free', and proclaimed the year of the Lord's favour.

What does this mean for those who follow him? What guide does his programme provide for those who are members of his body? Who are the poor? Where are the 'broken victims'? Who are the 'prisoners'? What is the task of the Church in respect of them? Is it not the case that by helping to create, renew and sustain a just political system Christians can express love for the multitudes of people they will never personally meet?

More and more since the end of World War II questions of this kind have been touching the nerve of evangelical thought, and Evangelicals have been remembering earlier days. As a breed there is a proper pride in numbering historical figures like Wilberforce and Shaftesbury in the ranks, and in recalling nineteenth-century evangelical concern to abolish slavery, create factory legislation, and provide education.

113

Increasingly though, it has been recognised that social concern had declined into charitable activity, a work—no matter how admirable—dealing with symptoms rather than causes. This, indeed, ought to have been done, but without leaving undone the whole enterprise of attacking the foundation causes of social deprivation or suffering. But as evangelical influence declined in the Church, and as new theological trends and new scientific thought made their impact, so Evangelicals manned theological barricades to defend their view of Scripture and of salvation by faith through the atonement.

In due course, however, the tide began to turn in the life of Evangelicalism. Chastened, humbled, grown in wisdom, the movement survived and began to grow again. With this growth came a new sense of responsibility for the world and a new sense of confidence about the contribution it could make to the debate about national and global society.

The reasons for this are many and complex. A very recent survey of them, published just in time for the Congress by the Shaftesbury Society, is *Contemporary Evangelical Social Thinking—A Review* by Derek J. Tidball. 'The evangelical party cannot be considered in an environmental vacuum', he writes (p. 8). 'The necessity to grapple with post-war economic and social problems is as pressing an issue for this party within the Church as for any other party.' He goes on to mention, as further contributory influences, the rise of the social sciences in university faculties, the impact of the World Council of Churches' growing social and political involvement and 'the enormous impression made by theologies from the third world—theologies of hope, development, liberation, revolution and change' (p. 9).

'Since the Sixties', he continues, 'Evangelicals have continued to write on the issue of social concern. The two obvious characteristics of later years have been, firstly, diversification and secondly, divergence. The diversification is apparent in that some have written or spoken at a slightly more sophisticated theological level, while others have been prepared to write in detail about specific social issues ... The divergence has come in the theological arguments used and the conclusions reached' (p. 11).

The fact that social and political matters were on the mind and heart of Evangelicals of all kinds and from many lands came to the world's attention in 1974 at the International Congress on World Evangelisation in Lausanne. Clause 5 of the Lausanne Covenant dealt with Christian Social Responsibility and the doctrinal basis for this is summarised by Derek Tidball in this way: 'There is the doctrine of God as Creator and Judge, concerned with justice in his world. Secondly the doctrine of man, made in God's image. But the new features are the third and fourth bases. The third is that the message of salvation is one of deliverance from evil and evil is both personal and social in its expression. Lastly, social responsibility is seen as a mark of being a member of the Kingdom of God' (p. 24).

I make this rather lengthy preamble to a discussion of the Congress treatment of its third topic to indicate the point in church life at which the contents of *The Changing World*, volume three of the pre-Congress trilogy, made their entry. It was out of this background of Christian life and thought that the six authors and their editor, Bruce Kaye, made their contribution. It was from the same background that the Congress committee came to their very right decision to include the topic in the Congress agenda, and to commission the work. The topic may sound novel and strange to some, but it was in fact not only predictable but theologically inevitable. Sooner or later it had to be brought to the conscious attention of the Anglican Evangelical constituency. 'NEAC II' was the right occasion.

Nevertheless, discussion of the topic—of its inclusion in the agenda, of its implications for church life, of its impact upon evangelical unity, of its intellectual and academic challenge, of its relationship to the Bible—all discussion of this kind was at least as interesting and significant as the actual series of discussions which were built around the chapters of volume three. There may have been a lengthy run-up to the Congress debate: the books themselves were three years in the making, if one includes in that time-span all preliminary thought and discussion. But for many delegates, perhaps for most, actual discussion of such matters with fellow Evangelicals was a notable novelty.

'I don't want to sound pompous' said the Rev John Poulton (as if he could), 'but . . . ' and chatting into my tape-recorder as we trudged across the broad grass-lands of the Congress campus, went on to say that discussion of socio-political matters at the gathering reminded him by their enthusiasm of student debates. People, in his view, were glad to be launched into what he called 'an acceptable discussion', and for people with the corporate identity of Evangelicals this was important.

But it was not only zest which was apparent, he

thought. People were discussing 'without a lot of background and without a lot of information. And there is', he observed, 'a real rift between "Left" and "Right", between young and old. But the important thing was that they were glad they were discussing these kinds of issues.'

Referring to the clergy present he said that 'quite obviously this was something they wouldn't reckon to be doing back in their parishes and are glad to have the opportunity of doing it here in a real move forward and corporately'.

Taking a glance into the future he said that if there were to be a further gathering in ten years time 'one would hope that there will have been a lot of filling in so that we won't be so naive and naked when we come to the next one, but that discussion next time will be based on a lot more work in between'.

This is not to say that preparation for the debate had been skimped by the authors of the chapters of volume three. 'Power in Our Democracy', 'The Power of the Media', 'Education and the Law', 'Marriage and the Family', 'The Gospel and Culture', and 'Global Stewardship', were themes tackled with that degree of conscientiousness which is so characteristic of Christians of this ilk.

I asked Bruce Kaye what he had learned from his labours as editor of the volume, and the first thing he said in reply was 'Personnel'. He went on to explain that the Church has strong personnel resources available to it as it tackles such subjects.

'The research groups', he said, 'contained large numbers of very competent lay people who had real knowledge and skills arising out of their background and training in the areas which the chapters of the

117

book were trying to deal with. That to me was really important and fairly new in terms of evangelical thinking and working at social and ethical questions . . . I would dearly love to see these lay people encouraged to dialogue with the theologians and vice versa so that theologians are saved from inanities, and lay people are helped to think theologically about the knowledge of, and involvement in, social issues.'

The lack of expertise in discussing socio-political matters which John Poulton noticed among Congress members chimes in my mind with what Bruce Kaye said about the evangelical theological tradition. 'We aren't able to cope with the questions', he said. 'Our theology has been developed in order to defend and deal with other questions. We've got a good strong tradition about the atonement and christology, but in areas of social ethics we are not able to cope at the moment. Look at the formularies of evangelical societies. They don't speak to any ethical question. The Lausanne Covenant was a real breakthrough in this area. Norman Anderson has been a pioneer. But he is not a theologian and I think the theologians should follow his lead.

'Central to ethical questions', he said, 'is the interpretation of Scripture. We are committed to the authority of Scripture. But the interpretation of it is not something we are accustomed to deal with very intelligently when it comes to social-ethical questions. We declare the Ten Commandments and don't know what to do with Leviticus.'

And this was where hermeneutics surfaced in that particular discussion. 'Anthony Thiselton', he said, 'has been moving people into areas which hitherto they have not really considered. We need to get more imagination and more wit about the way we interpret the Bible, and in ethics that is particularly important.'

Harking back to the long months of preparation for the Congress he made it plain that this matter of biblical interpretation was very much a challenge to those concerned with writing the chapters in his own volume.

'It came up time and time again', he said. 'I couldn't help observing that the contributors were using Scripture in the chapters in a somewhat uncertain fashion. Some felt confident that they were using it in the right way, and others were, I think, a little tentative, and some hardly used it at all. And that, I think, reflected a little bit of a difficulty.'

Certainly people are right to ask 'What is the connection between the Bible and socio-political matters?' It is obviously a question right in the forefront of leadership thinking. Oliver O'Donovan, who wrote the chapter about Marriage and Family Life, had a pertinent word for my hard-working tape-recorder on this subject.

'We have this belief', he said, 'that there are two ways of facing the problems of the world as a Christian. One is to look up a verse in the Bible on all possible occasions and to stop there. The other is to recognise that that's not good enough and to throw the Bible away and act by intuition. I don't think either are good enough. I think there are Christian ways of seeing things which we need to be trained to see by careful Bible study.

'There is a Christian, biblical view of marriage, for instance. One can't be simplistic about converting the biblical teaching about marriage into today's thinking, nevertheless it gives us the framework of thought.

'With regard to Prison Reform, Medicine, Abortion, Euthanasia, Marriage, Economics and so on: how does the biblical view of man in society cut here? How can we see what there is in the Bible and unpack its riches in thinking in an ordered way about this kind of thing?'

It is this refusal to divorce thought about social, political and ethical matters from deep biblical enquiry which promises to be the major contribution which Evangelicals can make to the world-wide debate.

But it will obviously not be a glib contribution, delivered in triumphalist manner. In socio-political terms Evangelicals are apt to be illiterate. There was a sense at Nottingham among some that primary education in the field had at last begun.

Bruce Kaye admitted: 'Sometimes we've been a bit too slick in the way we've dealt with the "understand-of-the-world" questions, and therefore, for most people I think it is the social ethics question which is the more biting and urgent one. People *don't* know how to explain their Christian life in the society in which we live, and so they withdraw their Christianity into something which isn't relevant to the world in which they live and so there's a strange kind of "acceptable hypocrisy" which is terribly demoralising to faith.'

'The social involvement issue', he stated, 'is now firmly on the agenda in a way which I don't think it has been before. And it's now known to be on the agenda. That's the key thing. The fact that volume three was a whole volume is very important, very significant.'

On the agenda it surely is. But people quickly let it

120

be known that the concerns of volume three only partially represented the problems which Christians must tackle. Clearly the questions tackled in its six chapters were never meant to represent a comprehensive breakdown of the world's problems, although the final chapter on 'Global Stewardship' had a pleasingly written survey of major world issues. There remained a wide range of topics which could have absorbed the energies of many other working parties and authors, and earnest conversationalists could be heard chatting together about Unemployment, Town Planning, Penal Reform, Welfare Services, Work and Leisure, Medical Ethics, and, perhaps more than most, the challenge of the inner city.

One wonders how the 120 strong group which got itself together to discuss the inner city would have impinged upon the Congress had Bishop David Sheppard, away in America at a Partners In Mission Consultation, been able to fulfil his original intention to be present.

Bruce Kaye admitted that with the passage of time the processes by which certain subject choices were made had become a little hazy. He could not quite recall how it was that the question of inner-city areas and its major questions for the whole of society had been left out of the final selection. It was, he conceded, a glaring omission. He was glad that it had not gone unnoticed, though he had hoped for stronger leadership on such matters from the rank and file in the give-and-take of the Congress.

Given that by choosing some topics the committee had perforce to exclude others, the six chapters represented a realistic beginning, on a reasonably wide front, to what is clearly destined to be an ongoing process of study.

As the Congress proceeded it became clearer to all concerned that the themes of all three books were deeply interrelated, endlessly intertwined. One simply cannot discuss the Lordship of Christ without discussing that over which he is Lord, whether it be church or world. So volume one's concerns underlay all of volume three's. And one cannot discuss the people of God without reference to their life and location. So volume two's concerns also underlay volume three's. And one cannot discuss the changing world meaningfully without reference to God and his Christ, nor to those whom God calls to stewardship.

This overlapping of themes shed light on many matters. Referring to volume one's doctrine of Christ, Bruce Kaye pointed out that this was crucial for the Christian's understanding of God's relationship to his world. Unless we begin to understand that relationship, we shall have little light to shed upon the ordering of the world's affairs. The purely theological question of God's relationship to his world, he observed, 'is the other side of the social ethics question. Social ethics are concerned with the way we, as followers of Christ, are involved in the world. The other side of that question is "What is God like who wills this will, and how do we understand his presence in the world in which we are living?" That's a vital question.'

The question, too, of how the vast amount of local grass-roots discussion required by socio-political matters can be programmed by the churches is addressed, at least in part, by much of the thinking contained in volume two's chapters about the church.

But more of that later.

One thing was clear from the start. The last people likely to be surprised by any remark about the ways in which the subjects of the three volumes overlap and interrelate would be the organisers. In his opening address John Stott urged those present to keep the three subjects together, for they belong together. They are interrelated, he suggested, because the Church must be under Christ, and a church under Christ must be a church for the world. It is called out of the world to be with him, and sent back into the world with his authority. And with characteristic simplicity he spoke of Christ's authority 'over the world into which he sends the Church'.

It was because the Congress members accepted this view, stated as it was with neatness and conviction, that they were able to adventure into the much less tidy, much less clear, much more uncertain fields of discussion about politics, education, family life, multi-racial community life, the conservation of the earth's resources, the deployment of its wealth, and so on.

It was swiftly apparent, however, that Christian charity was not going to muffle party-political convictions, and there was for me the novel experience of seeing devout brothers quivering with passionate dissent from views being expounded by other brothers, equally devout. Heads which had been bowed in pious prayer meetings were twitching around on stretched necks to see the owners of some voice expressing views which touched some quaking political nerve, or outraged some secular principle. Votes on amendments to the draft Congress statement showed on a number of occasions that adherents of the political Left were present in equal numbers to those of the Right, even though, as someone pointed out, 60 per cent of those ordering morning papers were having the *Daily Telegraph* with their breakfast.

With this honest, and occasionally rowdy, clash of opinion envisaged from the start, the organisers were clearly praying and believing that Christianity itself would prove to be the winner. Such prayer was heard and answered, but in the process those present had to rethink the nature of brotherhood, and without the syrupy pretence that being holy means total agreement about all things social and political.

The organisers' risk paid off in the event. People began to discover that their Christianity is something deeper than any set of political views. But some frank fears were acknowledged as affairs were proceeding. Particularly in view of the fact that it was not only political polarities that were involved, but also the exciting mix of 'charismatic' and 'non-charismatic' folk and formats.

'What the Congress really raises in my mind', said John King, the former editor of the *Church of England Newspaper*, and the author of *Evangelicals Today*, 'is what evangelical unity really means and what it's worth. If it means that we are agreed on highly spiritual things which don't lead to practical implementation, and if we find that we are no more agreed with each other than we were at the discussion I was at this afternoon, then we are bound to ask what kind of value do we place on evangelical unity? Is it a superficial thing, or is there more to it than that? This is the kind of fundamental question this Congress has raised.'

John Poulton said he believes that if Christians do

their homework (and field-work) over the next ten years, and if there then should be another Congress, further debate about social, ethical and political matters will be 'hairier'. 'It will result', he thinks, 'in a lot more confrontation. Whilst there may be guidelines there certainly won't be guidelines that will drive us all into one political camp.'

Perhaps this means, surely it must mean, that the signposts hammered into evangelical ground at Nottingham will, if followed, lead to greater stress as differences are more honestly debated. As John King asks: What is evangelical unity worth? Is 'Evangelicalism' big enough to hold together people whose political views are divergent? Will such divisions of opinion lead to splinterings off into politically like-minded cliques? Or will they drive brethren, who find themselves in political disagreement, into a deeper study of the Scriptures, and into deeper and more Christian fellowship? Will Christ truly be Lord?

Christians faced with such a challenge must pray for that deeper fellowship. But, as some observed, there may be stormy days ahead.

There is another factor, however, in the whole debate and that is the charismatic renewal. I asked Michael Harper whether the community life-style in which differences are either resolved or lovingly lived with, is in any way related to the current concern for social righteousness.

'The test of Christianity', he said, 'is love for the brethren. Christians who have experienced the power of the Holy Spirit in their life become much more social in their concern. Whether we like it or not we are conditioned by the culture we have come up from, and I would have said that the tendency in the charis-

125

matic movement—at least until about 1970—was to be "White Anglo-Saxon Protestant", very much to the Right politically, being suspicious of the World Council of Churches and the Roman Catholic Church.

'A change has come about in the 1970s for two reasons. First, the Roman Catholic influence: the Roman Catholic renewal began very significantly in the northern part of the United States in the milieu of the University of Michigan, Ann Arbor, and in Pittsburg. They're very "gritty" people, these RC's I've found, and they tend to be, as far as Americans can be, more to the Left than to the Right, and they have challenged the charismatic movement in America to the social issues. And there have been others saying—and I have myself been saying it for some time—that as Christians we need to be concerned about the world and its condition, and not only concerned about rescuing people from the world.'

Will the effects of the charismatic renewal permeate the whole area of debate where political hackles normally rise? No doubt it will play its part. But the great hope for increasing clarity of debate with increasing charity of spirit surely rests upon the nature of the Word of God, the Word by which the worlds were made, the Word which knits together into one all the concerns for Christ, his Church and his world.

The achievement of Nottingham is that it has woven these areas together into the conscious thought patterns of Evangelicals.

The Debate

The Congress office was still packing up, the

heroes, concerned to make available for the press the scissors-and-paste version of the Congress statement, were still hard at work at St John's College, Bramcote, and my car was still panting in the drive after a two-and-a-half hour dash back to Liverpool when the relevance of Nottingham thinking got sharply underlined in my mind. Behind the telephone in the Rectory was an accumulation of mail, and prominent amongst it was a copy of a letter sent to all Merseyside clergy from Merseyside church leaders. It was encouraging local churches to organise public meetings about the imminent Merseyside County Council Elections, and to invite all local candidates to attend. Together with that letter was a copy of one addressed by the same church leaders to all local candidates. The second paragraph read as follows:

'We welcome the emphasis in public debate on the needs for jobs, housing and facilities in the Inner City, but we think it fair to question whether there is the political will to bring in such policies and to give continuity to them. Too frequently policies have been reversed in favour of the party's methods before there was time for them to bring about effective change. We ask candidates of all parties publicly to commit themselves to continuity in policies which will offer better resources to Inner-City areas. No doubt there are not many party gains to be made in this way; the majority of seats in the Inner-City area are not marginal. That is why, as church leaders concerned with all types of areas on Merseyside, we believe it right to press this massive human need on you.'

Probably the last piece of paper I picked up at NEAC was one bearing the 'Declarations of Intent'. And declarations numbers 9, 10 and 11 were all brought joltingly to mind by this 'episcopal round-robin'. They are: (9) 'We repent that we have been backward in facing issues of social responsibility, and in accepting social and political involvement in obedience to Christ, and we acknowledge that we have a duty to take action in our local situations for the well-being of our neighbour and against all that is unjust, dehumanising, sub-Christian, and dishonouring to God.' (10) 'Because we have often been ignorant and ill-informed Christians through neglect of study, we commit ourselves to develop realistic programmes of Christian learning as a regular part of the life of all our churches.' (11) 'We repent of the narrowness of our Christian interest and vision, and we undertake to maintain informed and active concern for the worldwide spread of the Gospel, for the stewardship of the world's resources, and for the cause of welfare and justice among all men.'

The letter behind my telephone had been signed by the Bishops of Liverpool and Chester, the Roman Catholic Archbishop of Liverpool, and Auxiliary Bishop of Shrewsbury, the Chairman of the Liverpool Methodist District, the Moderator of the Mersey Province of the URC, the North-West Area Superintendent of the Baptist Union, and the Divisional Commander of the Salvation Army.

In addition to reminding me in practical terms of the relevance of NEAC thinking, it brought, some time later, the thought that NEAC was not so much leading the way as trying to help people catch up. Certainly as I sat through discussions about the matters touched on in volume three, aware of the intense commitment to a debate which seemed to be breaking new ground for so many, I had the strong feeling that I had 'been there before'.

What in fact was coming to mind, like some lost Atlantis surfacing once more, was a whole pattern of inter-connected memories of similar discussions entered into under the aegis of 'Call To The North'— a movement transformed into 'The Northern Consultation For Mission' only two weeks after the end of NEAC.

The socio-political implications of mission, considered ecumenically, and pondered in terms of God's Word to his world, had increasingly been the concern of many study groups in the north whose activities had been loosely related to one another through the CTN organisation. It was no accident that ten days after NEAC ecumenical officers and kindred spirits who used to meet under CTN auspices, were together at Scargill House, Yorkshire, thinking on these very things. As I sat with them there, a trifle drowsy from the drive in an absurdly overloaded week, my mind occasionally drifted off and persuaded itself that it was in Nottingham and at NEAC.

Concern for socio-political matters, I reflected, had been sharpened and focused on a wide front since the Archbishops' call to the nation in the autumn of 1975. It just is not possible to ask 'What kind of society do we want?' and 'What kind of people must we be?' (in order to have it) without involving true spirituality in socio-political thought.

The 'episcopal round-robin' behind the phone on my return from NEAC reminded me how far things have already moved in some quarters.

But even if there was, for some of us, a *déjà-vu* feeling about the NEAC socio-political debates, there was also something which was wonderfully fresh. It

129

was not just the freshness of an interest which was taking some delegates by surprise, it was the freshness of a liberated conscience. No doubt there were many present who had discussed politics a great deal in other contexts—most probably with people who did not share their Christian faith. Here there was the release of discussing the matter with those who deeply held the same faith, and who mostly spoke in the same religious dialect, people with whom they were spiritually at home. There was a delicious surprise for some that this was now an 'OK Thing' for keen Christians to do. The freshness of that realisation, in what was a genuinely warm and loving fellowship, gave something special to a lot of the debate.

John Gladwin, Tutor at St John's College, Durham, discussed the views expressed in his chapter 'Power in our Democracy', and reacted to the comments sent in beforehand by a good percentage of the delegates. Accustomed as one is to seeing politicians engaged (on television and elsewhere) in doing the same sort of thing, it was an intriguing experience to see in John Gladwin a novel blend of mild-mannered courtesy and clear-headed pugnacity. Answers were direct, sometimes blunt. There was some good verbal quarter-staff play, with differing viewpoints cracking together like stout oak staves. At intervals there were flashes of good humour, moments of corporate affection. Here and there individuals quivered with frustration as pent up feelings failed to find release.

One brother who began the session with a seat near my own, spent most of the time restlessly on foot, hand shooting up from time to time, but with so many eager to participate never getting the longed-for nod from the chair.

Now and again, as some point was made or rebutted, there would come the muted bray so characteristic of the British disporting themselves at politics. It was rather like play-time in the Commons.

But did the exercise indicate that we were in at the birth of new trends in political thought? Were there signs of a new direction being taken by quickened consciences and Christian conviction?

One way of trying to answer such questions is that of putting together the theological principles most frequently appealed to, with the themes most often pursued, with the issues most usually tackled.

In his booklet, referred to above, Derek Tidball summarises those three areas of thought in this way. The theological principles are those of God's creatorhood; of man's creation in God's image; of the social as well as the personal implications of salvation; of social concern as being a mark of membership of God's kingdom.

Theology, laying emphasis on those four points, most frequently discusses the themes of man's dignity, the institution of government, the obligation to work, and the role of legislation.

The specific issues earmarked for particular comment by Derek Tidball, in the light of this, are race, revolution, and the urban world.

It would be an intriguing exercise to think through the inter-relationships of those three categories, and to apply the fruit of such thought first to the selection of themes in volume three of the Congress books, and then to the record of their debate as represented by the Congress statement.

Such an enterprise is, alas, beyond the scope of this piece of instant journalism. But the suggestion may be a worthy one, if only, in the process of discarding it, someone might find a more fruitful line of enquiry.

There is a much simpler and shorter answer to the question 'Were new lines of Christian political thinking apparent in the discussions?' And that answer is 'No'. Comment and debate was predictable, and followed well-worn lines. But to say that new thought was not discernible is not to say that none is on the way. It is in the nature of seeds to be small, even to be invisible.

And for many there was a certain satisfaction in feeling the powers of biblical truth coming to attention in three great battalions behind the following propositions which were offered as a theological framework to the discussion of 'Power in Our Democracy'.

'(a) Government is an activity ordained by God and is called to the exercise of power in response to the demands of justice, love and freedom.

'(b) Government requires institutions and structures for its work. Whilst these ought to serve the godly purposes of government, they can, and sometimes do, turn power to evil, and oppressive purposes.

'(c) The divine ordinance of government does not predetermine any particular form or structure and so these must always be regarded as capable of change or reform.'

The predictable generalities which emerged from the debate should not be under-rated. The call for Christians to be involved in the process of government at all levels, and for this to be generally regarded as a vital part of Christian vocation, is basic. So is the call to create the possibilities of in-depth political education, and to facilitate the processes by which the whole local community may be involved in decision-forming debate. Above all the need for a new vision for human life, available in Christ through the Church, is an ideal well beyond the prison walls of platitude.

A number of small-group discussions brought up valuable thoughts which were untested in the fuller debate but which no doubt would have gained wider approval. The local church was called upon to be alert to local events and issues as part of its care for the community. Involvement in local politics should not be left only to individuals but Parochial Church Councils should also consider the possibility of comment. Suburban churches were asked to relate their life to that of churches in deprived areas, and Christians were called to consider choosing to live in urban areas.

Concerning industrial disputes, members urged support for secret ballots, and in the life of industry as a whole, consultation at all levels was advocated.

An alternative statement was drafted by a group which wished to make similar points from a more Right-wing stance. After some polite disagreements it was decided to include the whole of this together with the agreed text, as the expressed views of a small *ad hoc* gathering.

A little bit of drama fittingly marked the debate about the power of the media. Festival of Light Director Raymond Johnston's chapter had laid emphasis upon such matters as the concentration of power in relatively few hands, the need for proper accountability on their part, and the need to understand the effects of the mass-media so that they may be both employed and criticised in an enlightened way.

Well represented at NEAC were Christians engaged professionally in the arts and media, and as Raymond Johnston and interviewer Michael Saward talked through the questions raised by the chapter, this group and those who also felt that the creative aspect of literature and the arts *vis-à-vis* the media had been neglected, decamped to hold their own debate. So the Congress was treated to the news that while Tories and Socialists were happily battering each other in one debate, those discussing the more gentle matters of art and drama were in open rift.

The report was a trifle misleading. The groups, having had a chance to chew over their complementary concerns, came together again and produced an effective item for the Congress statement. In it they spoke of the opportunity for creativity provided by the media; the need to study its effects; the importance of appreciating its political and economic power.

In paragraph 2(c) the resultant document makes a statement of real power which reconciles the concerns of both (temporarily) polarised groups in a positive way. I quote: 'We acknowledge that wide differences of belief and life-style can co-exist in a democratic society such as our own. Nevertheless we believe it is both right and essential to set our faces against all that dehumanises men, women and children and we therefore urge the media to set their goals in such a way as to ensure that they encourage not only the pursuit of legitimate material satisfactions, but also the heroic and sacrificial instincts in both individual and society . . . ' and then comes, what to my mind is the major insight. 'This means that the elements of both light and darkness, and of good and evil in human nature are explored in such a way as to help mankind to understand and pursue the path to true maturity. As Christians we believe that such a path is supremely traced in the life and teaching of Jesus Christ.'

The statement calls on Evangelicals to explore the rich artistic heritage of world culture and to play their part in its creative development, setting new standards in their work.

The hope was expressed that local churches would encourage the development of artistic skills, that the wider Christian community should subsidise people of talent in these fields, and that work be invested in the theology of communication.

Deep thought and study certainly remains to be done. The division of opinion revealed by the 'walk-out' may have been amicably resolved within the life of the Congress, but it marks an area of concern which needs further attention according to John Poulton, a member of the group whose thinking contributed to the writing of the chapter being discussed.

'It reflects', he said, 'something which in the writing up of Nottingham I hope will be looked at quite closely. A fairly sharp division between people who live in the artistic world and are unaware of the commercial interests which are manipulating them, whether they like it or not, and others who aren't necessarily artistic themselves and who are aware of those interests. The wider issue, which is so incredibly important, is the really deep division between those who have been really agreeably surprised and responsive to the (Congress) morning sessions which have not been biblical expositions (they were in fact dance

135

and drama presentations of biblical themes), and those who have grumbled away saying "OK, there's a place for drama, mime, audio-visual aids, but don't let these swallow the steady firm print-medium style teaching of the gospel which has been the traditional evangelical contribution to the Church." In the assessing of Nottingham we're going to have to look closely at what I think will have to be more of a balance, more of an understanding. It is important for the media divergencies to be worked out.'

The discussion about 'Education and the Law' encountered some pre-Congress trouble in that many people thought the debate was to be about education, whereas in fact the real topic was law, and the Christian's understanding and use of it in society. Education was picked as an illustrative topic in order to earth the discussion. Perhaps it was too cleverly picked, because education being in its present state of flux and debate people were apt to be more interested in that than in law. On the other hand the combination certainly widened the agenda and with so many other themes untouched this was a plus.

It was stimulating to hear David Harte, lecturer in Law at Newcastle University, say that 'secular law is itself defective, and necessarily arbitrary'. 'It is our Christian responsibility', the ensuing statement goes on, 'to influence law so that it promotes social justice and allows people to hear the Gospel and to live in as close a manner as possible to Christ and to one another and in conformity with God's moral law.'

In applying law to education the statement says: 'It is not possible to deduce from the Bible any system of education which should be provided by law. There was frank recognition that Christians differ over the justification for comprehensive education and independent schools. Whatever the pattern existing at any time, Christians should be committed to making best use of it and to improving it . . . We feel that study and research is needed on the educational implications of new legislation.'

Commenting on the current debate concerning the needs of industry in our society, it was stated that this was a proper concern but 'these needs must not be allowed to determine the direction of the school curriculum. We call on all Christians to affirm that schools are not assembly lines but communities in which children develop in a context of discipline, order and individual care.'

The debate was also concerned with what it called the 'hidden curriculum'—the assumptions, structures and policies in education which reflect an overall view of man. Christians should work for a 'hidden curriculum' reflective of a Christian view of man.

It was noticeable that in debating such matters Congress members seemed more assured and competent than in debating political matters. This clearly reflected the generally middle-class composition of the membership and the professional involvement in education of many of those present.

One of the heartiest and most rumbustious sessions was that conducted by Oliver O'Donovan in the face of Brandon Jackson on the subject of 'Marriage and The Family'. Matters of homosexuality, divorce, marriage preparation and support, parenthood, varying man–woman roles in society, and the single life all came up for debate. This is a subject which bears very directly upon congregational life at parish level, and carries an array of challenges to the whole Church.

I asked Oliver O'Donovan whether the Church's attitude to sex and marriage formed any kind of a backdrop to a non-Christian public's awareness of who and what is speaking when the gospel is being preached.

He replied: 'For every word preached that is effective in people's consciousness there lies some kind of vision of the Christian life and community in which the word is going to spring. People notice one another's family life—they notice whether families get on, whether they are happy and warm in their relationships, whether the children are happy, whether husbands and wives really love each other. People feel family warmth in some churches and have been drawn into the faith by it. Some people, also, have been put off the gospel by a negative attitude, a sense of forbiddingness and hostility towards sexuality and family life.

He went on to say that he hoped the Congress would start people 'thinking afresh about how their church ministers to people in the whole sphere of sexuality and family life, and that lay delegates will ask "Have I a ministry here?" Marriage preparation has always been one of those sacred clerical tasks in the Church, and I think one has to see it in a very much wider light as the whole Church ministering one to another in the sphere of marriage concerns— offering help to married couples, helping them understand their marriages, helping the unmarried to prepare for marriage, helping those who are not called to marriage to live in their single state.'

'Singleness', he observed, 'is an achievement. One has to work for it as one has to work for a happy marriage.'

138

David Bronnert, vicar of St John's, Southall, a racially mixed parish, himself a former chairman of the Evangelical Race Relations Group, made some deeply moving points in a 'low profile' response to questions directed towards his chapter on the 'Gospel and Culture'. He is glad to live in a multi-racial community, he finds that it is an enrichment of life and not a deprivation. With many others present he gladly accepts 'that the United Kingdom is and will remain a pluralistic society' and he longs for 'a church that is enriched in its life by the varieties of cultures and races'.

One member of the small early morning prayer group to which I belonged was very concerned about one aspect of this on the following day. He thought it to be one thing that people should accept the plain fact that we live in a pluralistic society, and quite another that we should 'gladly accept' that it will remain so. He was not at all concerned with limiting immigration, or with matters of colour. He accepted Britain as a multi-cultural, racially diverse family of people. But he felt that the gospel and the Christian mandate to preach it, meant that the Church could not by its very nature be happy to think of Britain remaining pluralistic in religion. We should work, he strongly felt, for the day when there will be 'one Shepherd and one flock'.

Over against that very proper Christian concern was the basic point about religious freedom which David Bronnert dealt with lucidly in debate and which the Congress Statement expresses in the following way: 'We rejoice in our national tradition of religious freedom and tolerance, for the Bible makes it plain that God has given to people the precious gift of choice. We do not wish to lose this freedom for ourselves, or to deny it to others.'

In his chapter (p. 122) David Bronnert observes that 'religious liberty is a tender plant and can easily be destroyed; evangelical Christians are a small minority and would very soon suffer if it were lost.'

It was clear, however, that mission is as mandatory in a multi-racial, pluralistic society as anywhere else, but that it must express itself in service and dialogue as well as in evangelism. This, it was clearly seen, is something about which Christians can be ultimately confident for 'it belongs to the very nature of the gospel that the Church is built across cultural, social and racial barriers' (vol. 3, p. 125).

Questions of religious education in a racially mixed community, the use of redundant church buildings by people of other faiths, and the question of multi-faith services were all debated with compassion as well as conviction. How to love and serve others in the Spirit of Christ without betraying the uniqueness of Christ and obedience to the Gospel, was the splendid theme of a moving debate.

Within the debate came an appeal for attention to be given to the Church's role in urban areas. Failure there, it was said, 'is a failure to follow the example of our Lord himself, and constitutes disobedience to him'.

In new paragraphs on the theme added to this section of the (then) draft Congress Statement, it was roundly asserted that at the time of the Keele Congress 'we thought our failure was one solely of communication. Ten years later we realise that our failure is more basic than that. We must "put flesh" on the facts of the gospel and make Jesus real to the inner-city man . . . We need also to see and to act upon the fact that our message is not just for man as an individual . . . but for the whole of the universe, for the society of men, the structures of his living, all his relationships, for man's wholeness both personally and socially.'

The vast concerns deployed throughout the chapter on 'Global Stewardship' grasped the imagination of many people. Presided over with irenic expertise by Philip King, General Secretary of the South American Missionary Society, the multi-lateral concerns of a Christian conscience in a complex world defy easy analysis, and it would be unjust in so partial a review as this to pretend to summarise such a wide-ranging debate. The presence and involvement of many acute and informed minds was evident throughout. The concern, which is now widespread in society, about matters like population growth, poverty, exhaustion of resources, the growing gap between the world's rich and poor, and the information explosion in the Third World, indicates the power of the mass-media in communicating such things, and the multiple forms which concern for them are taking throughout the Church.

Technical and political expertise were apparent in the discussion, with representatives of missionary societies revealing a high degree of Christian statesmanship.

The need for global concerns to influence individual life-style, parish policies, governmental affairs, and international relationships was enunciated in principle and spelt out in varying degrees of practical detail.

Throughout my recollection of it all runs the thread

141

of something said by Sir John Lawrence in his book *Take Hold of Change*; 'All lands and every age are woven into one web' (p. 23).

There was some degree of heart-searching about the lack of emphasis on mission, and the place within it of evangelism. Mission was something everyone, the Congress leadership very much included, had wished to stress. The whole concern for the world had been seen in terms of mission, it was observed. But, aptly, somebody else quoted Bishop Stephen Neill to the effect that 'when everything is mission, nothing is mission'.

So it was that the Congress Statement under this heading began with the following assertion, one that was felt with authentic evangelical passion: 'This Congress reaffirms that mission is a worldwide task and that our primary duty as stewards of God's grace is to proclaim Christ, relating him to all forms of human need. Only through him can men marred by the fall, be radically and permanently changed and receive eternal life. The great commission gives global responsibilities to all churches at all times and at all stages of their development.'

The Future

'We are told ... that we are living in a post-Christian age. I do not think so. I believe, on the contrary, that we are indeed entering a period of drastic change, but that in the end the Church will be found to be stronger than before. I am not saying that religion or the churches will emerge unchanged. Far from it. The change will be as great as it is possible to conceive without a destruction of essential continuity—as great as the change between Judaism before the captivity and Judaism after the return . . .' (Sir John Lawrence, *Take Hold of Change*, p. 3).

'The Christendom that some of us grew up in is changed beyond recognition and there can be no going back. But there will be a going forward into what I must call the second Christendom' (ibid. p. 65).

'We are like people on a ship in mid-ocean. We cannot get off, but we can change course. We must start from where we are' (ibid. p. 38).

I took Sir John Lawrence's little book with me to Nottingham to read, as a kind of 'obbligato' to the surrounding debate. As it happened I had more than enough to read, and one post-Congress correspondent in the *CEN* complained about being 'drowned and smothered by the endless printed papers'.

Nevertheless, not having to take the dog for a walk, I had a moment or two at the end of each day, and the reading of it reminded me afresh of the way in which the whole Church is alive with theological, social and missionary speculation. Just as the world is going through a period of unprecedented change, and thinking men the world over are trying to grasp the principles of it, so too the worldwide Church is grappling with the principles of change in response not only to the world but also to the Word of God.

The last year has seen the publication of a number of books on this theme. Stephen Verney's *Into the New Age* talks about the complexity of this process of change. In it he sees three essential features: first, diversity, in which individuality is affirmed and explored; second, interdependence, in which free and self-aware individuals co-operate and come to depend upon each other; third, relationship of

143

mature individuals, interdependently related to a central authority—God.

At NEAC one could see ample evidence of all three processes at work—people asserting their individuality, finding new ways to fellowship, responding corporately to God.

Another recent book is Howard A. Snyder's *New Wineskins*, sub-titled 'Church Structure in a Technological Age'. He points to some startling similarities between the first century AD, when the gospel circled the known world, and the present very different age. Conditions which made the gospel so drastically relevant then are present now. But the 'old wineskins' of ancient church organisation need replacing by structures suitable for this new and still rapidly changing age. He explores the notion that a 'small-group structure' is best suited to embody and express the life of the Church in an urban and technological world.

Again, these considerations were well represented in the proceedings at NEAC, with debate about the form and functions of church life, local and national, endorsing the relevance of such thinking.

When up against some mental blockage in preparing a sermon I find that one way to resolve things is to stand back from the work and ask myself what my prayer for the hearers actually is. When I know what I am praying for them, usually, I know what I want to say (if not always the way to say it). So it was that when the Archbishop of York was addressing the opening meeting of the Congress I achieved total concentration (always easy when he is speaking) at the point when he disclosed what it is he prays for as he thinks of the Church in this time of change.

He is praying, he said, for four things. (1) A new generation of 'militants' who will study the emergent pattern of things and plan ahead for action based on the Word of God. (2) A new generation of thinkers, for 'there is no hope for a church which stops thinking'. (3) A new generation of contemplatives, for one man of prayer can change the psychology of a whole nation. (4) A new generation of prophets who will hear the word of the Lord and apply it to the issues of the day.

What signs did NEAC afford of such a prayer being answered? And what sign-posts for the future were being painted in the minds of those present?

Well, to be fair, the Congress was not structured with the needs of contemplatives in mind and to say that one was not struck by immediate evidence of their presence in strength is neither here nor there. But the worship was emphatically whole-hearted. The fact that it was usually rowdy, too, and that Michael Baughen had to work hard in the initial stages of the final eucharist to impress upon all present the need for reverent silence, was more amusing than indicative of any lack of absorption in the mysteries of God.

The contemplative element in such an affair was to be found in the way people like Jim Packer talked about God and Christ in the theological sessions. One cannot speak about the nature of Christ's self-consciousness, as Dr Packer did, without betraying the inner-life of a contemplative spirit.

There was, obviously, rather more evidence of the emergence of the 'militants', the 'thinkers' and the 'prophets'. The structure of the Congress and its selected concerns saw to that. The published papers which delegates were able to read before arrival, and the responses of their authors to Congress questioning, served to indicate the kind of militancy, thought and prophecy active in the hearts and minds of some of the leadership.

I was able to explore this a little further in the limited opportunities there were to talk to some of them. It was a minute exploration but the yields were encouraging and significant.

In connection with the concerns of 'militants' and 'prophets', what is the immediate way ahead in terms of theological thought and training? Bruce Kaye had a clear view of this.

'In terms of our theological resources we are very thin on the ground in this area,' he said. 'We really only have one person in all evangelical theological colleges whose main speciality is ethics. There are others who teach doctrine, and as a side to that teach ethics, or who teach historical theology and as a side to that teach ethics. That is a somewhat unsatisfactory situation. It confirmed my experience in the Grove Ethics Group that it is very hard to find people in the evangelical constituency whose major academic specialisation is in the area of ethics.

'I would dearly love to see the colleges encouraging young men who have got first degrees in the social sciences and who then go on to do theology, to study ethics. And already, since editing volume three, I have tried to sort through prospective students and encourage them in this area.'

He believes that money must be spent on in-depth study and research. 'The evangelical societies which have funds ought to set aside money so that people can devote themselves to heavy-weight moral

146

theology, moral philosophy, ethical study and examination. We really do need a lot of study and research and that needs to be inter-disciplinary in character. It must be basically theological, but the theologian needs to be informed by the social science disciplines. We won't get this done, though, without funding. Funds are given to all sorts of things,' he added, 'and this is an area in which we must be prepared to spend money.'

He wants to see projects like the Shaftesbury Society developed and expanded. The fact that the latter is inter-denominational has special importance at a time when some Free Church Evangelicals feel a little estranged from Anglican Evangelicalism.

'I'd like to see conferences, study sessions, seminars, symposia in that area of work conducted under the general umbrella of the Shaftesbury Society on an inter-denominational basis rather than on a specifically Anglican one,' he said.

'I would also dearly love to see the Grove Ethics Group continue and develop its publications activity. They produce very useful books—they stimulate people to think and are simple enough.

'Also, such going concerns as the Mayflower Family Centre in Canning Town, and the "Christians in Industrial Areas" group have really got to be encouraged and supported further so that we can not only evangelise in the urban situation, but so that we can also understand how Christianity works in that situation. The lack of shop-stewards and the like at Nottingham is a reflection of our lack of social spread.'

If that suggests one way ahead, theologically, what is the way ahead in terms of applying an educated Christian mind to such matters as, for example, economics?

Bruce Kaye referred to 'the one man' who in evangelical theological colleges specialises in the teaching of ethics. That man was Oliver O'Donovan of Wycliffe Hall, Oxford, who, while this book is being printed, will be packing his bags for Canada to take up an appointment at Wycliffe College, Toronto (and then there'll be none?).

I asked him how he thought Christian ethics might tackle economic issues. He was illuminating in reply.

'When Christians discuss the broad issues of economic ideology, you still find them discussing it in the old antithesis between capitalism and socialism which has been bequeathed to us. The world has said to us: "Here is our issue. This is the thing which has got to be discussed. Discuss it in these terms please, and opt for one or the other."

'To me, a really deep Christian understanding of man is just not going to accept the way that discussion is run. And it's going to say: "I'm sorry. The question's put wrongly." I want us to be involved in putting back the questions in a much better, and a much wiser, and much more profound form to the world, and say: Now if you saw man differently you might see that the question isn't that at all. The question is rather how a man stands in regard to his work and his freedom. And the Bible has things to say on these things.

'What certain Christians have been saying for centuries—before Marxism was ever heard of—is that Christianity values freedom and freedom of action, just like the capitalist does. But he does not see that as a licence to exploit or even be selfish. The freedom the Christian values is the freedom to give

148

and to create something for his brother, not the freedom to create something for himself. This is the first re-writing of the premisses of capitalism.

'The option you're given is "every man for himself" on the one hand (freedom), or every man controlled and his freedom taken away from him so that people don't exploit one another. Now that's not the option God has given us. We've been given the option of exercising our freedom for one another. And that's one of the fundamental "givens" of economic ethics.

'The second way in which the Christian might want to rephrase these options is like this: Capitalism has traditionally seen work as a purchasable commodity. "I sell you my work, like I sell you my house, at the best bargaining price I can get for it." But the Christian must put a question mark against any view which sees work as a disposable commodity quite apart from the person who's working. I don't hire "labour". I hire a "labourer", a person, to be a "fellow labourer". I don't want a commodity... I want fellow labourers.

'This is one of the fundamental philosophical questions we must put to a society which is used to putting things in Free-Market terms. Even the Left wing are thinking of things in Free-Market terms now: "What can I get for my labour?" And Left-wing unions join Right-wing people to call for Free-Market bargaining because "we can sell our labour for much more if we're clever and skilled."

'It's just not God's way of looking at it. We are co-operative beasts.'

As Christians learn to apply their theology to the basics of our social and economic life they will surely find that the Church has a growing audience. 'When one thinks freshly,' said Oliver O'Donovan, 'and when one thinks freshly in a Christian way, people listen. People are always interested in seeing things new and seeing things freshly. This is something which one must do for the world.'

Fresh thinking and social commitment then, it is alleged, ultimately win an audience for the gospel, and are true partners of evangelism. Is this borne out by experience?

One man likely to have views on such a matter is Bishop David Sheppard. As Congress members were settling into their rooms at Nottingham University he was settling into Louisville, Kentucky, for a Partners in Mission Consultation organised by the American Episcopal Church. When he came back I asked him for his thoughts in this general area. His answer, prompt and direct, was coloured by his recent experience in the States.

'I always regard it as a great sadness when the Church splits into two camps in discussing mission, with one group concerned about matters of justice, community life, and political involvement, and another group concerned about spiritual matters and evangelism. This is a real issue in the American Episcopal Church. There was a time when the American Episcopal Church was unlikely to be taken seriously by those who feel themselves at the bottom of the pile in society. Now it is taken much more seriously, and this is due to the courageous stand its members have taken on matters of civil rights. It was a stand taken at great cost in terms of money and membership. It remains a live issue, however, because some of our American brethren in the Episcopal Church confessed to being what they called "battle-weary", and hoping that with notable achievements behind them they could get on with what they refer to as the normal work of the Church—meaning by that its worship and evangelism. Others see that there are many more matters of social need requiring their continued attention. And as consultants and "partners in mission", we felt we had to press upon them the need to do both: to pursue worship and evangelism, and not to flag in their concern for social justice.'

With thinkers and prophets involved on these fronts and, depending upon the quality of their work, gaining a hearing for the gospel, what of evangelism? And so far as the immediate future is concerned, what about that national mission which has recently been discussed and still more recently, it seems, dismissed?

Back to John Poulton, whose years as Executive Secretary of the Archbishop's Council for Evangelism gives him a better view than most of the factors involved.

Referring to his experience at NEAC he said: I've received support for the position which the discussion at national level has now got to: that the initiative in evangelism has now got to be locally based . . . regionally based at most. To try to do a national campaign would not properly reflect where people feel themselves to be. It's more of a low-key, low profile "let's work it out locally" sort of moment in their lives, and in the life of the Church.'

I asked him whether he thought that the ideas expressed about the Gospel and the Mission of the Church in volume two would give enough clues, to enough people, in enough time for a local church-based but nation-wide outreach to be conceivable in the near future.

'Our economic plight', he replied, 'is on the side of those who want to depart from tradition. A lot of the things said in book two are matters we are having to think about willy-nilly. What I think is going to have to happen now is much more experimenting, with much more realisation that while there may be national guidelines we're going to need a lot more experience under our belt. I'd like to think that in ten years' time we'd be in a position to compare different schemes of lay eldership, shared ministry schemes, and the like, as they have developed in different parts of the country. I'm sure from the New Testament that that's the way we shall arrive at the truth, rather than from trying to legislate for new schemes.'

Granted the need for pragmatism, what about that mission and what about evangelism now?

'The people to really pray for and expect from, from now on,' he said, 'are the diocesan bishops. As a church in a given county becomes an increasingly realised fellowship in the Holy Spirit and tries to do what is right in its own area, there is where we should expect the growth points to emerge.'

In this synodical age, then, is this throwing fresh leadership responsibility squarely back upon the bishops?

'I think so,' he replied. 'When I was listening to those who were moaning about the lack of cohesion in the C of E, and of how difficult it is to plan nationally, and so on, I became aware of the fact that this may really be a twentieth-century way of being very worldly—the "organisation man" way of thinking about the C of E! An industrial psychologist has reminded me that the smaller area in which people can feel loyalty is the one in which the best work is going to be done. This speaks of the need to make the diocese the real point of loyalty in the C of E, and far from playing down the bishop and the local church, this is where we ought to be putting our energies.'

Many streams of contemporary thought run into that point of view, and few will deny its cogency.

It is fair, however, to say that many at Nottingham were keen to see some nationally conceived proclamation involving mass rallies of the kind associated with, though not necessarily conducted by, Dr Billy Graham. It is equally fair, however, to observe that John Poulton's analysis does not rule out, but on the contrary allows for, such rallies to be organised regionally where there is the appropriate regional will and consensus.

My own guess is that different opinions will continue to be expressed. Partner to that guess is another, that the sort of Evangelicalism declaring itself at Nottingham is not of a mood or temper to be split by differing opinions as to method. Evangelicals are more likely now than ever to accept that the needs are so vast, so multi-dimensional, that a multi-faceted missionary enterprise united by the one Spirit is more in accordance with reality, secular and divine, than any scheme capable of being master-minded by mere men.

Certainly if John King's assessment of his fellow Evangelicals is right, our fellowship is mature enough to take firm hold of the debate and to make of it something new to the glory of God.

Writing in the *CEN* on 6 May he commented on 'a decent lack of respect for elders and betters', 'infighting over procedural points', 'outraged professionalism', 'vigorous lobbying' and a 'rough adult determination', 'a freedom in worship' which all add up to 'grounds for thinking that today the evangelical movement has more bone, more muscle, more good red blood than it had ten years ago . . . What has been added is the gain in robustness, the determined advance, the freedom and maturity that show we have come a long way since Keele.' Earlier, in the 22 April issue he had written, 'It is difficult to see how such a movement can fail to put its imprint decisively on the Church of England and to begin to influence English society during the next ten years.'

That, surely, is a true word. But with increased influence there must needs be greater humility. And the instinct to applaud must be partnered by a will to repent.

I talked with Baden Hickman, religious affairs correspondent with the *Guardian*, widely known and respected for his in-depth reporting of church affairs over many years. He expressed the wish that Evangelicals would 'so shape their work, and their mission, and their ministry that they do not appear to be so abrasive to others of the faith. So often,' he said, 'that which they do appears to the outside world to be nothing less than an indictment of non-Evangelicals. They tend to walk as Big Brothers, themselves wanting to be the Prophets, the Mystics, the Teachers, the Thinkers—at times unable to see similar qualities in others. That, perhaps, is terribly sweeping, and unfair. But there is an abrasiveness towards other Christians. The intended penitence of Keele, which I'm sure in a way had a cleansing effect and created a solidarity, may have been overtaken by an exuberance and an enthusiasm which has reduced some of the benefits of Keele. If evangelical influence is greater now than for the last century it must be on its guard that it does not do harm with its new influence.'

I like to think that people attending NEAC would welcome those words, and absorb their good effects without loss but only gain to the enthusiasm of their commitment.

So to absorb faithful criticism as to grow in stature is one infallible mark of holiness, and it was about holiness that Dr Coggan spoke in his sermon in the great final Eucharist.

'Deep in our hearts we know this—that the most likely way that people will see Jesus will be in ordinary men and women like ourselves shaped to his likeness . . . In a few moments, in deep solemnity and silence, we shall receive the tokens of his passion, the broken bread and the outpoured wine. Perhaps he will say to us: "Pursue holiness—it is the one thing that matters above all others. Let me, by the power of my Spirit, fashion you, shape you, after my likeness." And if we dare find words to reply, we might put it like this: "Yes, Lord, I'm ready. Come as the wind. Come as the fire. Let me feel the full force of your blowing, and your burning. For their sakes I consecrate myself. Amen." '